Microsoft®
FrontPage®

Version 2002 Microsoft Office Family Member

plain&
simple

Greg Holden

PUBLISHED BY
Microsoft Press
A Division of Microsoft Corporation
One Microsoft Way
Redmond, Washington 98052-6399

Library of Congress Cataloging-in-Publication Data
Holden, Greg.
  Microsoft FrontPage Version 2002 Plain & Simple / Greg Holden.
      p. cm.
    Includes index.
    ISBN 0-7356-1453-9
      1. Microsoft FrontPage.   2. Web site development--Computer programs.   I. Title.

TK5105.8885.M53 H65 2001
005.7'2--dc21

                                                        2001044258

Printed and bound in the United States of America.

2 3 4 5 6 7 8 9   QWT   6 5 4 3

Distributed in Canada by H.B. Fenn and Company Ltd.

A CIP catalogue record for this book is available from the British Library.

Microsoft Press books are available through booksellers and distributors worldwide. For further information about international editions, contact your local Microsoft Corporation office or contact Microsoft Press International directly at fax (425) 706-7329. Visit our Web site at www.microsoft.com/ mspress. Send comments to *mspinput@microsoft.com*.

Acquisitions Editor: Kong Cheung
Project Editor: Mark Diller
Technical Editors: Jim Johnson and LJ Locher

Body Part No. X08-24319

*To all of my readers who use the World Wide Web
to improve communications and strengthen
connections with the other members of
our global community.*

Contents

6 Working with Tables 97

7 Using Navigation Elements 111

8 Using Frames 127

Acknowledgments

Like a good soup, a book takes on flavors from many places before it is ready to be savored. My agent Neil Salkind and founders David and Sherry Rogelberg of Studio B provide the container for the jobs that sustain me, and I continue to be grateful for their help. The publisher always provides the ingredients for a book but, in this case, I was particularly fortunate to have the contributions of my project editor, Mark Diller. Kong Cheung as acquisitions editor gave me the opportunity to do my second solo book for Microsoft Press. In addition, compositor Kerri DeVault prepared the manuscript; artist Mike Kloepfer achieved pleasing and easy-to-digest presentations of screens and task steps; and technical editors Jim Johnson and LJ Locher made sure there weren't any mistakes in the final product. Copy editor Holly Viola edited and proofread the text, and Shane-Armstrong Information Systems crafted an index that makes the contents easy to find.

It is the broth of the soup that holds it together, and I count myself fortunate to receive many forms of support from many family members and friends. My parents, as well as my brother and my sister and their families, are there for me in many ways, as are my friends Ann Lindner and Betty Contorer. As far as fuel to bring out the best in me personally and professionally, I'm particularly indebted to my spiritual community, Jewel Heart (a Tibetan Buddhist meditation and study group based in Ann Arbor, Michigan). My two daughters, Zosia and Lucy, spice up every moment of every day. I have found working on this book to be both delicious and nutritious and, like any good cook, am eager to share the bounty with my readers.

About This Book

If you want to get the most from your computer and your software with the least amount of time and effort—and who doesn't?—this book is for you. You'll find *Microsoft FrontPage Version 2002 Plain & Simple* to be a straightforward, easy-to-read reference tool. With the premise that your computer should work for you, not you for it, this book's purpose is to help you get your work done quickly and efficiently so that you can get away from the computer and live your life.

No Computerese!

Let's face it—when there's a task you don't know how to do but you need to get it done in a hurry, or when you're stuck in the middle of a task and can't figure out what to do next, there's nothing more frustrating than having to read page after page of technical background material. You want the information you need—nothing more, nothing less—and you want it now! *And* it should be easy to find and understand.

That's what this book is all about. It's written in plain English—no technical jargon and no computerese. Most tasks in the book take no more than two pages. Just look the task up in the index or the table of contents, turn to the page listed, and there's the information you need, laid out in an illustrated step-by-step format. You don't get bogged down by the whys and wherefores; just follow the steps and get your work done with a minimum of hassle.

Occasionally you might have to turn to another page if the procedure you're working on is accompanied by a "See Also." That's because there's a lot of overlap among tasks and I didn't want to keep repeating myself. I've scattered some useful Tips here and there, and thrown in a "Try This" or a "Caution" once in a while, but by and large I've tried to remain true to the heart and soul of the book, which is that the information you need should be available to you at a glance.

Useful Tasks...

Whether you use FrontPage at home or on the road, I've tried to pack this book with procedures for everything I could think of that you might want to do, from the simplest tasks to some of the more esoteric ones.

...And the Easiest Way to Do Them

Another thing I've tried to do in this book is find and document the easiest way to accomplish a task. FrontPage often provides a multitude of methods to accomplish a single end result—which can be daunting or delightful, depending on the way you like to work. If you tend to stick with one favorite and familiar approach, I think the methods described in this book are the way to go. If you like trying out alternative techniques, go ahead! The intuitiveness of FrontPage invites exploration, and you're likely to discover ways of doing things that you think are easier or that you like better than mine. If you do, that's great! It's exactly what the developers of FrontPage had in mind when they provided so many alternatives.

A Quick Overview

Your computer might have come with FrontPage preinstalled, but if you do have to install it yourself, the Setup Wizard makes installation so simple that you won't need our help. So, unlike many computer books, this one doesn't start with installation instructions and a list of system requirements.

Next, you don't have to read this book in any particular order. It's designed so that you can jump in, get the information you need, and then close the book and keep it near your computer until the next time you need to know how to get something done. But that doesn't mean I scattered the information about with wild abandon. I've organized the book so that the tasks you want to accomplish are arranged in two levels. You'll find the overall type of task you're looking for under a main section title such as "Adding Text to a Web Page," "Working with Tables," "Using Navigation Elements," and so on. Then, in each of those sections, the smaller tasks are arranged in a loose progression from the simplest to the most complex.

Sections 2 and 3 cover the basics: starting FrontPage and exiting the program, working with FrontPage's different ways of viewing a Web page file, and finding an Internet service provider (ISP) that can take full advantage of FrontPage's more advanced features. You'll also discover FrontPage's built-in Help system as well as other ways to troubleshoot problems if you encounter them. You'll move on to create your first FrontPage-based Web—first you'll create a one-page Web as well as an "empty" Web. You'll then learn how FrontPage can create a complete Web through its templates and wizards. You'll give your Web a professional look and feel by applying a preconfigured Web page design called a *theme*. Finally you'll learn how to save and close your new Web.

Section 4 is all about one of the most important aspects of creating Web pages—entering the words yourself, copying and pasting your contents from other Office documents or other Web pages, or inserting a file. You'll use FrontPage's tools for making your contents readable, including its built-in spelling checker, find-and-replace feature, and character and paragraph formatting options. You'll learn how to create bulleted and numbered lists and to break a Web page with dividers. You'll assign styles and develop style sheets to give your Web a consistent appearance. Finally you'll discover how to preview and then print your Web pages so you can check them before they go on line.

Section 5 shows you how to take advantage of the World Wide Web's graphical nature. First you add images to your pages. You'll learn how to add files from FrontPage's extensive clip art collections. You'll work with the primary Web page image formats, GIF and JPEG, and get some experience cropping, resizing, and moving images so they balance your words and other contents. You'll add some special effects to your images, including clickable areas called hotspots. Then you'll use FrontPage to add sound and video files to make your Web a truly multimedia affair.

Sections 6, 7, and 8 all examine ways to make your Web pages easy to read and navigate. Section 6 lets you work with tables, which give you many options for organizing and arranging Web page contents. Section 7 explores another fundamental aspect of Web page design—hyperlinks, which enable visitors to your Web site to move from one location to another with a click of the mouse. You'll learn how to link from one location to another in the same Web page and how to link to a new Web page or an e-mail address. You'll create shared borders—sets of hyperlinks presented as clickable buttons and that appear the same on multiple pages. You'll also work with FrontPage's Navigation View, which gives you a visual way to organize all the links in your Web. Section 8 delves into FrontPage's ability to divide individual Web pages into frames, which help visitors click from one page to another and view different types of content at the same time.

Section 9 shows you how FrontPage's Web Components can make your site dynamic, interactive, and up-to-date. With just a few mouse clicks, you add features that normally require sophisticated programming to implement. You begin by creating hover buttons, which encourage visitors to click on your links. You even learn how to generate some income for your Web site by managing banner ads that other businesses can display on your pages. You'll discover how Web components make your site searchable, and how they enable you to display interactive spreadsheets, interactive charts, and counters that record the number of visits to a Web page. Some Web components that are new to FrontPage 2002 even give you the ability to display real-time information on line, including the latest news headlines and maps so that you can direct visitors to particular locations. A new component even helps you create an e-commerce Web site and sell your products on line through an interactive sales catalog or an online auction.

Section 10 shows you how to make your Web pages interactive through the use of forms. First you learn how to assemble a form quickly through FrontPage's templates and wizards. Then you ex-amine the structure of forms so you can design them yourself from scratch. You'll add common data-entry elements such as text boxes, check boxes, option boxes, drop-down boxes, and more. Finally you'll explore one of the areas where FrontPage really stands out—processing the data your visitors send to you, formatting the form results, and sending the user a confirmation page.

Sections 11 and 12 deal with more advanced topics. Section 11 explores options for administering a Web site—changing Web and proxy settings, adding notes and comments, changing margins, and changing the title and other page properties. You'll learn how to examine and edit the HyperText Markup Language (HTML) code for a page. You'll learn how to preview, publish, and update your Web pages as well. In Section 12, you'll explore ways to customize FrontPage to match your working style. You'll customize toolbars, configure editors, and even detect and repair problems. These tasks may sound complex, but they're not—FrontPage makes them so easy that you'll sail right through them.

A Few Assumptions

I had to make a few educated guesses about you, my audience, when I started writing this book. Perhaps your computer is solely for personal use—e-mail, surfing the Internet, playing games, and so on. Perhaps your work allows you to telecommute. Or maybe you run a small home-based business. Taking all these possibilities into account, I assumed that you'd either be using a stand-alone home computer or that you'd have two or more computers connected so that you could share files, a printer, and so on. I also assumed that you had an Internet connection.

Another assumption I made is that—initially, anyway—you'd use FrontPage just as it came, meaning that you'd view your Web content in Normal view, with the default type fonts, and with the Status bar options displayed at the bottom of the window. In Section 7, you'll learn how to use Navigation View, and in Section 12, you'll explore HTML View. Also in Section 12, you'll learn about hiding the status bar, displaying the task pane when you start up, and other customization options. However, because my working style is somewhat traditional, and because FrontPage is set up to work in the traditional style, that's what I've described in the procedures and graphics throughout this book.

A Final Word (or Two)

I had three goals in writing this book:

- Whatever you want to do, I want the book to help you get it done.

- I want the book to help you discover how to do things you *didn't* know you wanted to do.

- And finally, if I've achieved the first two goals, I'll be well on the way to the third, which is for this book to help you *enjoy* using FrontPage. I think that's the best gift I could give you to thank you for buying my book.

I hope you'll have as much fun using *Microsoft FrontPage Version 2002 Plain & Simple* as I've had writing it. The best way to learn is by *doing,* and that's how I hope you'll use this book.
Jump right in!

Getting Started

Microsoft FrontPage 2002 is designed to enable you to create and edit individual Web pages and then organize them into full-featured, professional-looking Web sites for either personal or business use. You can create a family Web page or a Web site for your workgroup at your office. You can even start up a new Web-based business by creating a sales catalog with FrontPage and an online resource—Microsoft bCentral—with which it is closely integrated. Regardless of the specific use you have in mind, FrontPage is a versatile program you can use to get your content on the Web.

FrontPage is one of the most powerful programs of its kind. Yet it's also user-friendly software that's designed for use by both newbies (newcomers to the Web) and experienced Webmasters alike. The program has a number of wizards (step-by-step processes) you can use to create entire Web sites or individual pages as well as Web components (software add-ons) that can give your site interactive, dynamic content. You also have the freedom to create Web pages from scratch, giving you the flexibility to build any personal or business site you need.

This section of the book covers the basics: starting or exiting FrontPage, creating a FrontPage-based Web, signing up with an Internet service provider (ISP) that will make your pages accessible on line, and finding help and advice if you need it. There's also an overall view of the FrontPage window, with labels for the most important parts of the program. You can use that image as a touchstone for learning more about FrontPage.

FrontPage 2002 at a Glance

Microsoft FrontPage gives you a wide selection of tools for creating and organizing Web sites. The place where all the magic happens is the FrontPage window. The window is often divided into three or four sections that you can add or remove easily.

You can think of the first three sections (the Views bar, the Folder List/Navigation Tree pane, and the main display area) as different lenses for looking at the contents of a Web site. The fourth section, the task pane, presents you with hyperlinks to many common tasks.

The title bar displays the location of the current Web.

Menu bar

Minimize/Restore/ Close boxes

Toolbars

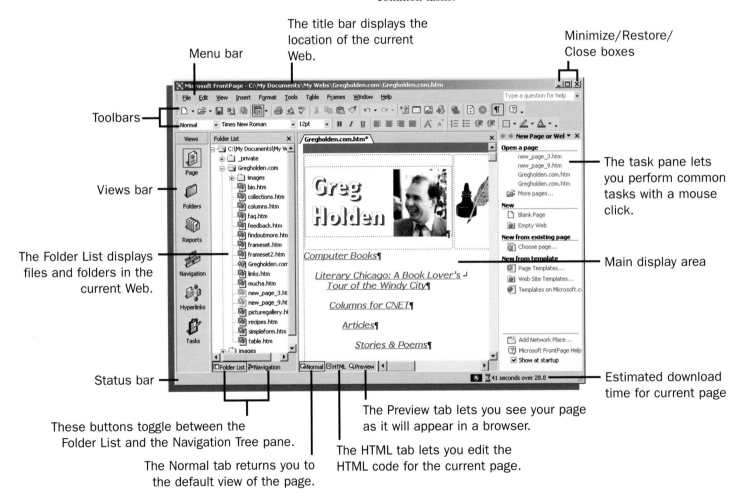

Views bar

The task pane lets you perform common tasks with a mouse click.

The Folder List displays files and folders in the current Web.

Main display area

Status bar

These buttons toggle between the Folder List and the Navigation Tree pane.

Estimated download time for current page

The Preview tab lets you see your page as it will appear in a browser.

The HTML tab lets you edit the HTML code for the current page.

The Normal tab returns you to the default view of the page.

The FrontPage Views bar gives you the chance to look at your Web site in a variety of ways. Upcoming sections will explore the different views in more detail, but here's a quick overview of what the Views bar buttons do:

● Page: lets you view and edit Web pages.

● Folders: All files and folders included in the currently displayed Web are displayed in the Folder List. The contents of the currently selected directory appear in the main display area.

● Reports: presents you with a Site Summary containing information about the currently displayed site's content, including hyperlinks and images.

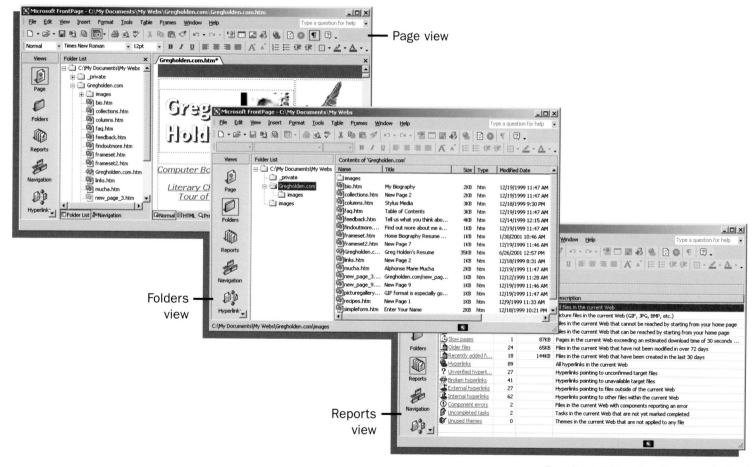

Page view

Folders view

Reports view

- Navigation: displays a graphic representation of all the pages in the current Web site and how they are linked to one another.

- Hyperlinks: illustrates how pages in your site are linked to one another. Click on a page in the Folder List, and the links associated with that page are shown in the main display area.

- Tasks: enables you to create and manage tasks for the Web you're working on.

SEE ALSO: The tabs beneath the main display area give you different views too. See "Adding Text to a Web Page" on page 43 for more information on previewing a page with the Preview tab, and "Viewing and Editing HTML" on page 204 for more information about the HTML tab.

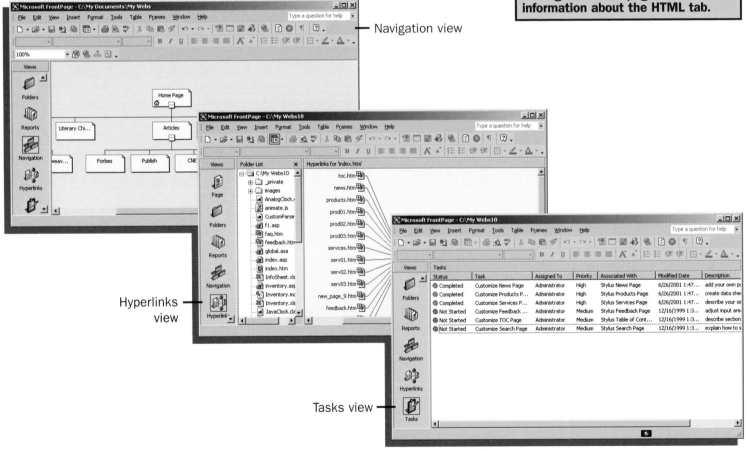

Navigation view

Hyperlinks view

Tasks view

What Is a World Wide Web Site?

The World Wide Web (WWW) is the best-known and most powerful medium for transmitting information via the Internet. Other media such as e-mail and newsgroups are popular, but they lack the capabilities that make the Web so influential—its interactivity, its multimedia components, and its hypertextual nature.

It all starts with a document called a Web page. At its most basic level, a Web page is a text file that is written with a set of formatting instructions designed to present words, images, and other material in a way that can be displayed by Web browsers. Two examples are Hypertext Markup Language (HTML) and XML (eXtensible Markup Language). A Web page document is saved with filename extensions (.htm or .html) and HTML code that identify it as a Web page. To view the words, images, colors, and multimedia contents, you need a Web browser such as Microsoft Internet Explorer. The Web browser reads the HTML code for the page and displays it on your screen. The HTML code can also contain Uniform Resource Locators (URLs) that specify the locations for other HTML documents.

A Web page document contains text, but it can become a lot more effective by including many other types of content as well. Web pages contain colors: each page has a background color, and individual words and phrases can be assigned colors as well. You can also add spot color—color that only appears in a specific area—by using Web page elements such as tables, as you'll discover in "Working with Tables" on page 97. Graphic images and sound and video files also contribute to the Web's unique nature.

Web pages can also be interactive. They contain hyperlinks, which let you jump from one location to another with a single mouse click. A set of Web pages that is interconnected by hyperlinks and that is produced by a single person or group for the same purpose is called a Web site. A Web site usually has a home page, which welcomes visitors and contains hyperlinks that lead visitors to related pages.

To create a Web site, you need to learn HTML or XML—or use a Web editor to create pages with buttons, menu options, tabs, and other user-friendly elements. That's where FrontPage comes in: it enables you to assemble a home page and other pages, add the hyperlinks that join one page to another, and create graphic elements that give your site a consistent identity.

Starting and Exiting FrontPage

Now that you've got an overview of FrontPage's working environment, it's time to start using the program and creating your first Web pages. Before you get started, you've got to start the program.

You've got a couple of options for starting up FrontPage—you can choose FrontPage from the Start menu or double-click a desktop shortcut you've created.

Start FrontPage

(2) Select Programs.

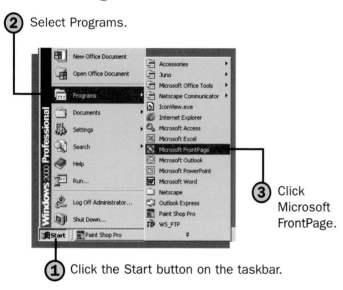

(3) Click Microsoft FrontPage.

(1) Click the Start button on the taskbar.

TRY THIS: You can add FrontPage to your Start menu, which can save you a second or two if your Programs menu is as crowded as mine. Right-click the taskbar, choose Properties, and then click the Advanced tab in the Taskbar And Start Menu Properties dialog box. Click Add. Follow the instructions in the Create Shortcut Wizard to add FrontPage to the Start menu.

TIP: You can rename a shortcut by right-clicking it, clicking Rename on the shortcut menu that appears, and then typing the shortcut's new name.

Create a Shortcut for FrontPage

(2) Select Programs.

(3) Right-click Microsoft FrontPage.

(4) Select Send To.

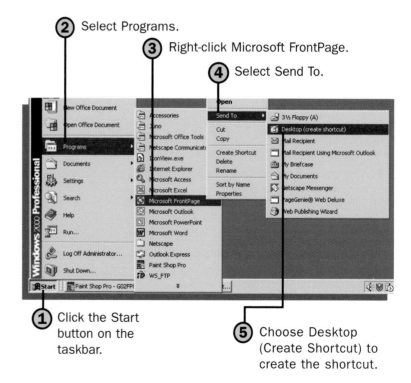

(1) Click the Start button on the taskbar.

(5) Choose Desktop (Create Shortcut) to create the shortcut.

Exit FrontPage

(1) Click the Close button in the upper right corner of the currently open FrontPage window.

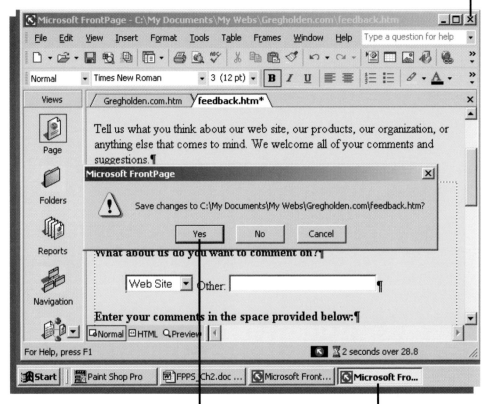

CAUTION: If you have more than one Web open at a time and you want to quit FrontPage altogether, choosing Exit from the File menu won't actually cause you to exit FrontPage. You need to click on the Close button or choose exit from the File menu for each open FrontPage Web.

SEE ALSO: For more information about closing open Webs, see "Creating a New Web" on page 23.

(2) If FrontPage prompts you to save your work, click Yes.

(3) If you have any other FrontPage Webs open, click on their taskbar buttons to restore them to normal size, and then click on the Close box.

Changing the View of Your Web

The various panes that subdivide the FrontPage window—the Views bar, the Folder List, the Navigation Tree pane, and the main display area—give you different ways to view your site's content. You should feel free to add or remove panes as you wish so that you can work with Web content more easily. Also try resizing panes and closing them, either by using the Views menu or each pane's Close box.

Change the Views Bar

① To Hide the Views bar, right-click anywhere within it and choose Hide Views Bar from the shortcut menu.

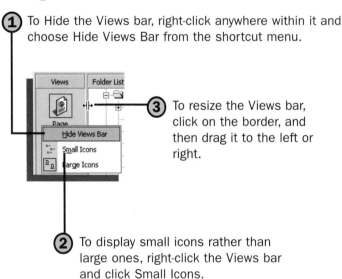

③ To resize the Views bar, click on the border, and then drag it to the left or right.

② To display small icons rather than large ones, right-click the Views bar and click Small Icons.

Use the Folder List

① Double-click a file displayed in the Folder List box to display that document in the main display area.

② Click a plus sign to view the files within a folder.

④ To close the Folder List, click its Close box.

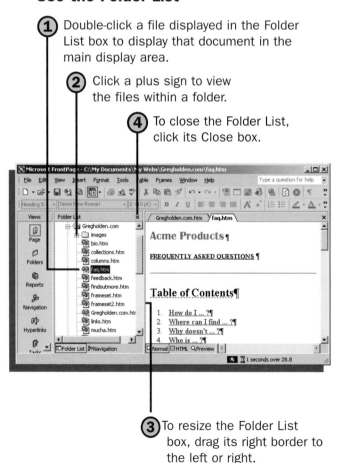

③ To resize the Folder List box, drag its right border to the left or right.

Use the View Menu

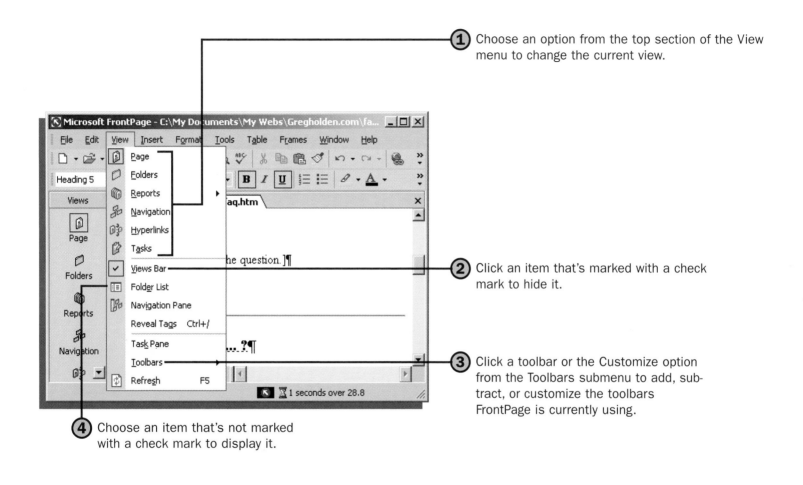

(1) Choose an option from the top section of the View menu to change the current view.

(2) Click an item that's marked with a check mark to hide it.

(3) Click a toolbar or the Customize option from the Toolbars submenu to add, subtract, or customize the toolbars FrontPage is currently using.

(4) Choose an item that's not marked with a check mark to display it.

TRY THIS: Want to learn HTML? Choose Reveal Tags from the View menu. The HTML commands (called "tags") for each part of the current page are displayed.

TIP: Click the Toggle Pane down arrow in the Standard toolbar to toggle between the Folder List and the Navigation Tree pane.

Finding a Host for Your Web Site

In order for your pages to appear on line, you need to sign up with a Web hosting service. Many ISPs host Web sites for their customers, and Windows' built-in Internet Connection Wizard can help you find them. Make sure the host you choose supports the FrontPage Server Extensions 2002. When the FrontPage Server Extensions 2002 are present, you can use FrontPage's full range of features to set up pages that are searchable, to create discussion Webs, and to design Web page forms.

Use the Internet Connection Wizard

1 Start the Internet Connection Wizard by clicking Start, pointing to Programs, pointing to Accessories, pointing to Communications, and then clicking the Internet Connection Wizard.

3 Step through the wizard until you reach the screen where the wizard connects to the Microsoft Internet Referral Service. Click on the name of one of the providers located by the Internet Connection Wizard to find out more information about it and then sign up if you're interested.

2 Verify that the I Want To Sign Up For A New Internet Account. (My Telephone Line Is Connected To My Modem.) option is selected, and then click Next.

Find a Dedicated Web Host

(1) Start up Internet Explorer, and go to the Locate A Web Presence Provider (WWP) page (*www.microsoftwpp.com/ default.asp*).

(2) Click on a hyperlink to find out about a suggested Web host that supports the FrontPage Server Extensions 2002.

CAUTION: Some Web hosts charge extra fees for use of the FrontPage Server Extensions. (Microsoft bCentral does not, however.) Check with your provider, and shop around for a hosting package that includes them at an affordable rate.

TRY THIS: If you have products that you want to sell on line, choose Web Component from the Insert menu. Click on bCentral Web Components, and then select bCentral Commerce Manager Add-In. The add-in lets you create a catalog that is hosted on bCentral's site. As a FrontPage user, you can post up to 25 items for free on bCentral.

(3) If you want to use FrontPage to set up an online business, go to bCentral's Web site (*www.bcentral.com*) and sign up for a hosting account on the Features And Pricing page.

Getting Help in FrontPage 2002

There are lots of ways to get questions answered while you're using FrontPage. If there's something specific you want to do and you can't find it in this book, unlikely though that is, you can get help by asking the Office Assistant a question, by browsing through the Help files available from within FrontPage, or by going to the Web.

Get Help Using the Office Assistant

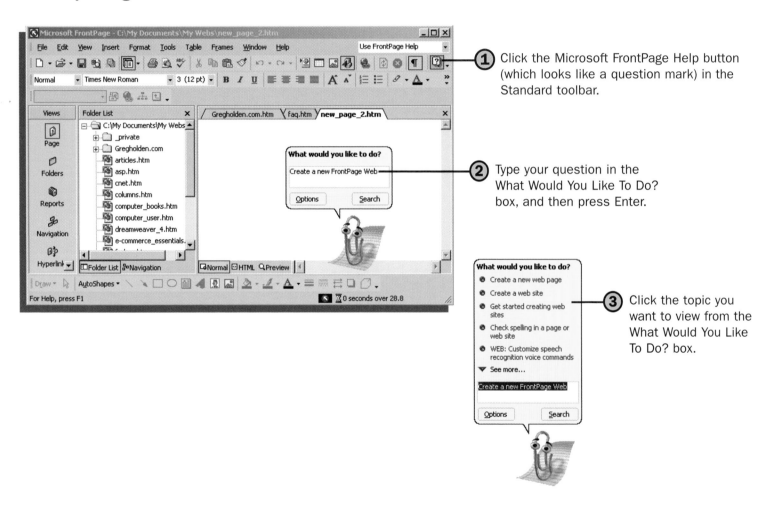

1. Click the Microsoft FrontPage Help button (which looks like a question mark) in the Standard toolbar.

2. Type your question in the What Would You Like To Do? box, and then press Enter.

3. Click the topic you want to view from the What Would You Like To Do? box.

Get Help on the Web

1 Connect to the Internet, and choose Office On The Web from the Help menu.

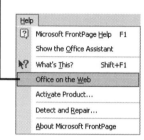

2 Follow the hyperlinks on the Microsoft Office Assistance Center Web site to find the topic you want.

> **TIP:** You can go straight to the Microsoft Office Assistance Center's page full of tips and tricks for FrontPage users by opening your Web browser and typing *office.microsoft.com/assistance/2000/TipsFrontPage.aspx* in the Address box.

> **TIP:** Don't just turn to the program's built-in Help files when you have a problem or a specific question. Browse Help through the Contents or Index tabs, or use the Answer Wizard when you need instruction on how to perform an intermediate or advanced task not covered in this book.

> **TIP:** There are some great resources on line that offer answers to FrontPage-related questions. FrontPage World (*www.frontpageworld.com*) has tips and tricks as well as a newsletter to which you can subscribe. Thomas Brunt's OutFront Forums (*www.frontpagewebmaster.com*) give you a place to meet other FrontPage users, ask questions, and get advice.

Consult Microsoft FrontPage Help

1 To get help when the Office Assistant is not active, choose Microsoft FrontPage Help from the Help menu.

2 Enter a question in the What Would You Like To Do? box on the Answer Wizard tab.

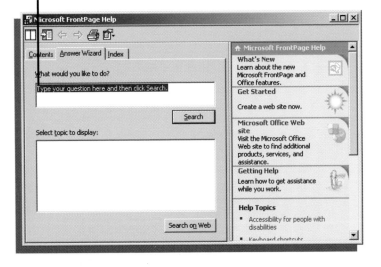

3 If the Answer Wizard can't answer your question, click the Contents tab.

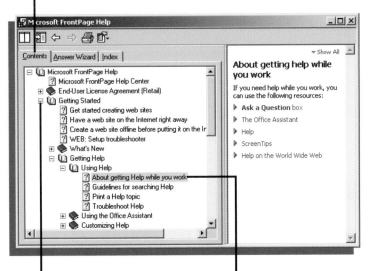

4 Click the plus buttons to expand the categories until a list of help topics appears.

5 Click the help topic you want to display.

TRY THIS: If the Office Assistant is not active, FrontPage Help opens immediately when you click the Help button. To disable the Office Assistant, right-click it and then choose Options from the shortcut menu. When the Office Assistant dialog box opens, clear the Use the Office Assistant check box and then click OK.

6 If the Contents tab doesn't list the topic you want, click Index.

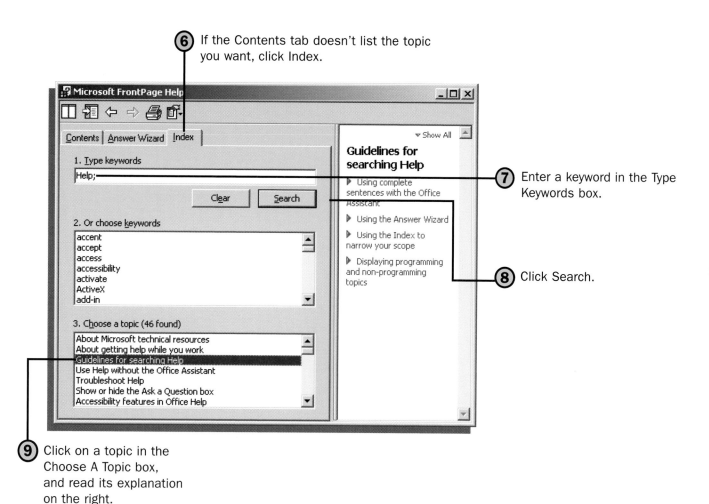

7 Enter a keyword in the Type Keywords box.

8 Click Search.

9 Click on a topic in the Choose A Topic box, and read its explanation on the right.

Troubleshooting Problems

Because you need to be on the Internet to browse the Web and publish your FrontPage files—that is, make them appear on line—you might run into problems with your modem or connection. You also might encounter software problems related to FrontPage, your browser, or the Web server. But together, Windows and FrontPage should be able to troubleshoot just about any problems you run into with either your hardware or with the program itself.

Try a Troubleshooter

(1) Choose Microsoft FrontPage Help from the Help menu.

(2) Click the Index tab.

(3) Type your text in the Type Keywords box.

(4) Click Search.

(5) Scan the extensive list of troubleshooting guides and other problem-solving utilities in the Choose A Topic box. Click one of the topics, and follow the instructions that appear in the right half of the Help window.

Turn to the Office Assistant

(1) If the Office Assistant is active, click the Help button to display its question box.

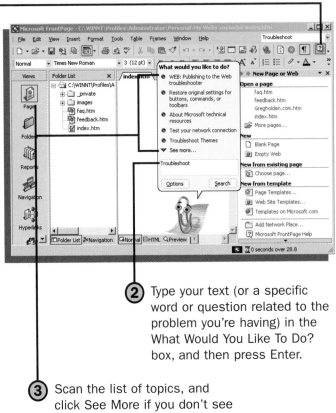

(2) Type your text (or a specific word or question related to the problem you're having) in the What Would You Like To Do? box, and then press Enter.

(3) Scan the list of topics, and click See More if you don't see the topic you are looking for.

Consult the Knowledge Base

1 Start up your Web browser, and connect to Microsoft.com's Search page (*search.microsoft.com/us/ SearchMS25.asp*).

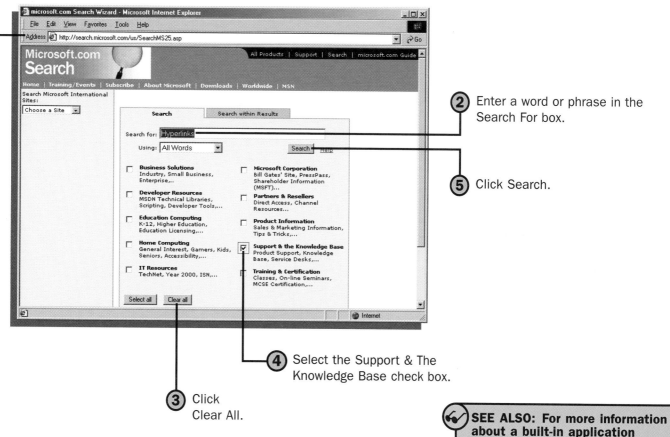

2 Enter a word or phrase in the Search For box.

5 Click Search.

4 Select the Support & The Knowledge Base check box.

3 Click Clear All.

SEE ALSO: For more information about a built-in application called Detect And Repair that can repair problems with FrontPage, see "Customizing and Maintaining FrontPage 2002 on page 217.

3 Creating a New Web

Starting to work with Microsoft FrontPage is a bit like buying a new car that comes with lots of slick electronic features. It takes some time to peruse the owner's manual and learn about every trick your new toy can perform. You don't start out with the advanced stuff right away. Instead, you start with what you bought the car to do: you drive it.

If you're a hands-on type that likes to work behind the scenes, you can use FrontPage as a blueprinting tool to create a set of Web pages that are linked to one another in a logical way. Then you can fill those pages with words, colors, or images.

But if you're not interested in the process of creating pages and linking them together, FrontPage can provide you with preconfigured templates or wizards. You can then edit your site to fit your needs. You can also create a visual look and feel for your site by your selection of colors, typefaces, and images.

This section shows you how to create a one-page FrontPage-based Web from scratch or by applying one of the FrontPage templates. You'll learn about the task pane and how it can speed up many of the tasks you perform most often. You'll discover how the FrontPage templates and Web wizards can automatically create complete Web sites for you to customize with your own content. You'll also get experience choosing and customizing one of FrontPage's many built-in Web design themes. Finally you'll learn how to open and close an existing Web and save it when you're done making revisions.

Creating a One-Page Web

Creating your first Web site might seem like an intimidating prospect. Not to worry; the FrontPage wizards and templates make it a breeze. Start by creating a FrontPage-based Web that contains a single page. You can then add new pages easily and link them into an interconnected Web site.

Open a Blank Web Page

② Begin typing and adding content to the new page after it appears in the main display area.

① Click the Create A New Normal Page button in the Standard toolbar.

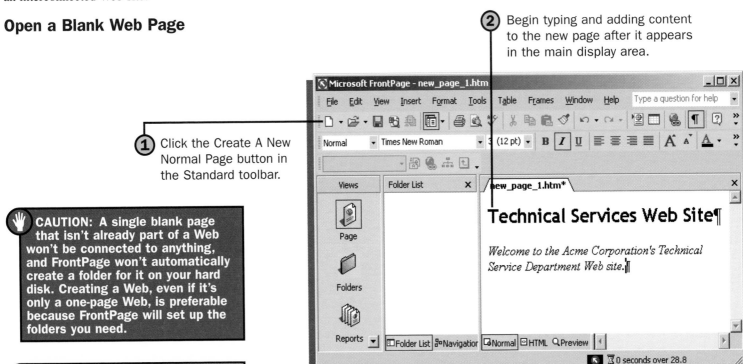

CAUTION: A single blank page that isn't already part of a Web won't be connected to anything, and FrontPage won't automatically create a folder for it on your hard disk. Creating a Web, even if it's only a one-page Web, is preferable because FrontPage will set up the folders you need.

SEE ALSO: The task pane contains shortcuts that enable you to quickly create a blank page, an empty Web, and a one-page Web. For more on using the task pane, see "Introducing the Task Pane" on page 28.

Choose a Page Template

(1) Click the down arrow on the Create A New Normal Page button, and then choose Page from the shortcut menu.

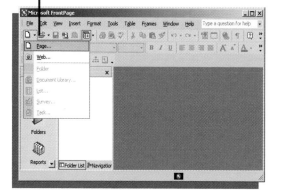

(2) The General tab is selected, but you can also click one of the following tabs:

- Click the Frames Pages tab if you want to create a page that is divided into frames.

- Click the Style Sheets tab if you want to create a page with predetermined type fonts and color styles for headings, backgrounds, and hyperlinks. When you select a template, a preview appears in the Preview area to the right.

(3) Click on the Large Icons button or the List button to choose between small and large icons.

(4) Click one of the page templates.

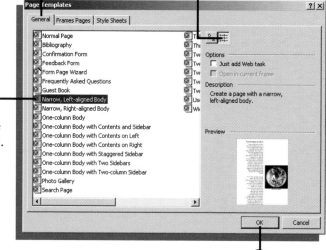

(5) Click OK.

Creating an Empty Web

An empty FrontPage-based Web doesn't have any pages in it. It functions as a placeholder for your Web when you're ready to assemble it. An empty Web has a folder that is assigned a generic name, "My WebsX," with X being a number that follows the most recent Web you've created. You can change this name if you want. The folder also has two subdirectories: _private and images. These directories are set aside to contain files your Web site will need.

Choose a Template

① Choose Page Or Web from the New submenu of the File menu.

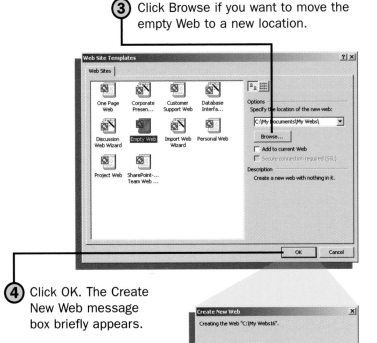

② Click Empty Web in the task pane.

③ Click Browse if you want to move the empty Web to a new location.

④ Click OK. The Create New Web message box briefly appears.

⑤ Click Folders to view the contents of the Web.

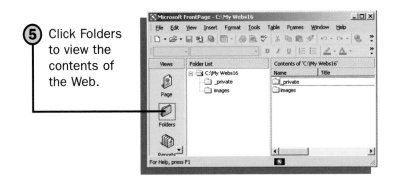

Add a Page

① With an empty Web open, click the Create A New Normal Page button.

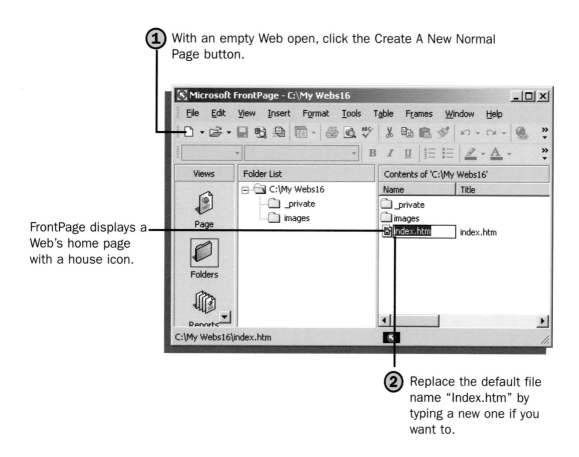

FrontPage displays a Web's home page with a house icon.

② Replace the default file name "Index.htm" by typing a new one if you want to.

! **TIP: The file name "Index.htm" or "Index.html" are special designations widely used for a Web site's home page.**

! **TIP: You can also add a new page by right-clicking on the Web's folder in the Folder List, and then choosing Page from the New submenu of the shortcut menu that appears.**

Introducing the
Task Pane ⊚ NEW FEATURE

The task pane is a new feature in FrontPage 2002 that enables you to perform common tasks by clicking buttons and links in the FrontPage window. Although you can make the task pane appear at any time by choosing Task Pane from the View menu, it usually appears when you choose a menu option and begin to perform a task.

The contents of the task pane vary depending on what you're doing at the time. The name of the current option appears in the bar at the top of the task pane. The New Page Or Web task pane allows you to quickly open an existing page, create an empty Web or a new blank page, or choose from Web site or Web page templates. The Insert Clip Art task pane appears when you choose Clip Art from the Picture submenu of the Insert menu. You can use this pane to insert small graphical files into your Web pages. The Clipboard task pane displays the contents of the Office Clipboard when you copy or cut something from an Office application. You can

Click on arrows to move
from one page to another.

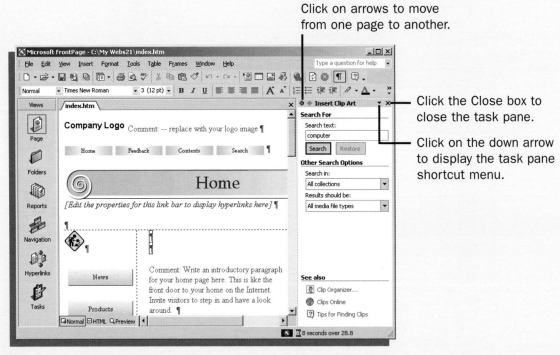

Click the Close box to
close the task pane.

Click on the down arrow
to display the task pane
shortcut menu.

easily paste any of these items into your Web. The Search task pane appears when you click the Search button in the Standard toolbar, select Search from the File menu, or select it from the task pane's shortcut menu. The Search task pane enables you to search through text in the current FrontPage-based Web, files on your computer, or documents on the Internet.

The left and right arrows on the task pane's title bar are only active when more than one page of information is dis-played. You can click on the arrows to move from page to page. Sometimes the FrontPage window isn't large enough to display all the links contained in the task pane. In that case, drag the scroll bar up and down to scroll through the entire contents. The down arrow on the title bar displays the task pane's shortcut menu, which enables you to choose between different task panes.

To save screen real estate, you can make task panes "float." In the task pane's title bar, hold down your left mouse button and then drag the task pane to place it wherever you want it on the screen.

The Clipboard task pane contains items that can be pasted into your documents.

Using a Web Template

Templates give you a head start when it comes to creating a FrontPage-based Web—you can concentrate on customizing the contents rather than on creating the documents themselves. A template consists of one or more documents that have pre-arranged headings, links, and placeholder text that you replace with your own contents. A page template contains the outline for a specific type of document, such as a Feedback Form. A Web template includes a set of related pages.

Choose a Template

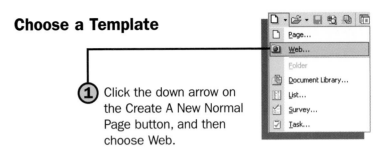

1 Click the down arrow on the Create A New Normal Page button, and then choose Web.

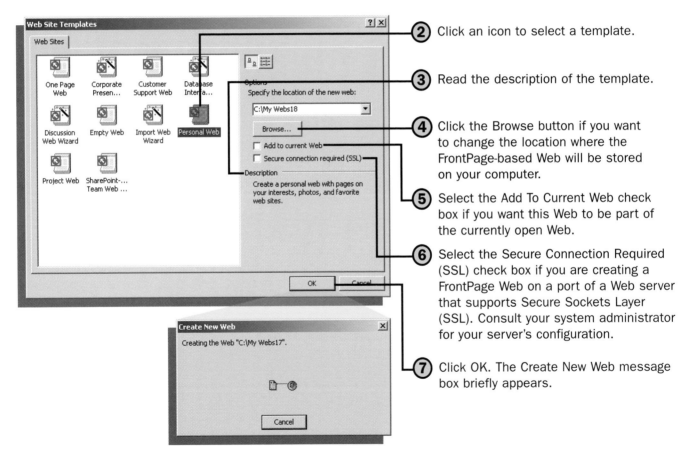

2 Click an icon to select a template.

3 Read the description of the template.

4 Click the Browse button if you want to change the location where the FrontPage-based Web will be stored on your computer.

5 Select the Add To Current Web check box if you want this Web to be part of the currently open Web.

6 Select the Secure Connection Required (SSL) check box if you are creating a FrontPage Web on a port of a Web server that supports Secure Sockets Layer (SSL). Consult your system administrator for your server's configuration.

7 Click OK. The Create New Web message box briefly appears.

View the Template

① Click Folders to view the files and folders created by the template.

② Double-click the home page, "Index.htm", to view it.

TIP: The Web template you create can either be a standalone Web or a sub-Web—a self-contained Web that is nested within another one.

③ Select the placeholder text, and replace it with your own text.

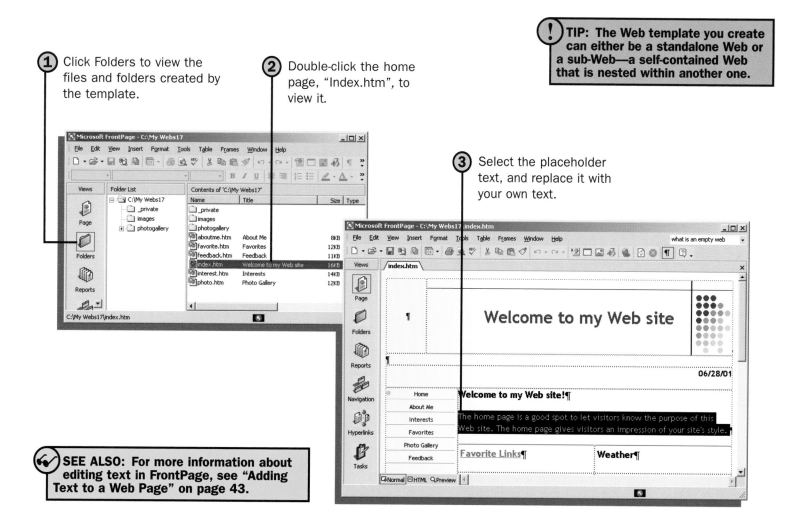

SEE ALSO: For more information about editing text in FrontPage, see "Adding Text to a Web Page" on page 43.

Using a Wizard

The FrontPage wizards lead you through the creation process by presenting you with options that allow you to configure the new FrontPage-based Web's contents without writing any HTML. You can click Finish at any time to have FrontPage finish the Web for you. The more detailed your responses, however, the more closely the Web will correspond to your wishes.

Choose a Wizard

You've got a couple of things to keep in mind when choosing a wizard. Wizards don't automatically create pages or Web sites. You've got to be prepared to take a few minutes to answer questions or choose options from those presented. To make the right choices, you should have a general idea of what you want the wizard to do for you. If you're creating a Web, decide what features the Web should contain and whether you want it to be part of the current FrontPage-based Web.

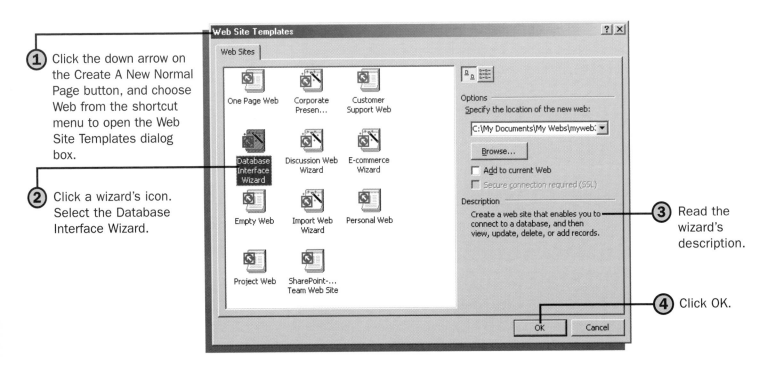

(1) Click the down arrow on the Create A New Normal Page button, and choose Web from the shortcut menu to open the Web Site Templates dialog box.

(2) Click a wizard's icon. Select the Database Interface Wizard.

(3) Read the wizard's description.

(4) Click OK.

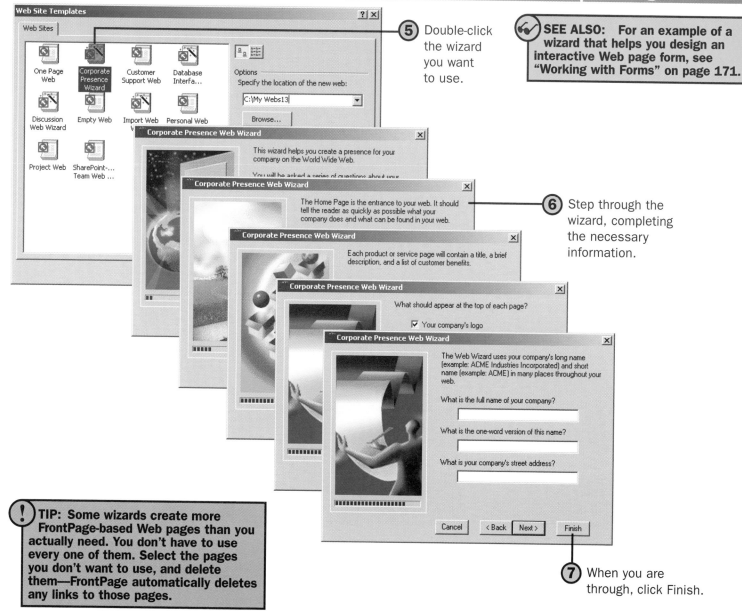

⑤ Double-click the wizard you want to use.

SEE ALSO: For an example of a wizard that helps you design an interactive Web page form, see "Working with Forms" on page 171.

⑥ Step through the wizard, completing the necessary information.

⑦ When you are through, click Finish.

TIP: Some wizards create more FrontPage-based Web pages than you actually need. You don't have to use every one of them. Select the pages you don't want to use, and delete them—FrontPage automatically deletes any links to those pages.

Using FrontPage Web Wizards

If you're new to creating Web pages, the FrontPage Web wizards will seem like friendly tutors, leading you step by step through the process. Think of a tutor who asks you a series of questions to determine what you want to accomplish. Then the tutor asks you to choose between sets of options—clicking buttons or filling in simple forms with your personal or business information. That's what a wizard does. Before you choose a wizard, it's helpful to have an idea of the general stages you'll go through so you can be prepared with your content beforehand.

Select the Features You Want

Typically, the first dialog box displayed by a Web wizard tells you that you'll be asked a series of questions about what you want your Web site to look like or how it should function. You move ahead by clicking Next, take a step backwards by clicking Back, or skip all remaining steps by clicking Finish.

The second screen of the wizard is where you begin to spin a set of pages into a FrontPage-based Web. You start by choosing from a set of check boxes that specify which pages the Web will include. The selected pages will be included in the finished Web. If you're uncertain whether or not you want to include a particular page, leave the option selected. It's easy enough to remove a page after the Web is created.

Organize Your Web Pages

Once you've specified the pages you want your Web to include, the wizard guides you through some organizational steps. First you name your Web and specify a storage location for it. Next you define the features your Web's pages should include. For example, in the Corporate Presence Wizard, you are asked which sections your home page should contain. In the Discussion Web Wizard, you identify the input fields your visitors will be able to use when they post articles. Before you know it, you'll have an organization for your Web.

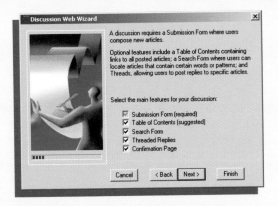

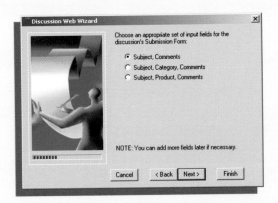

Specify Any Standard Page Information

After you've identified the pages you want and organized them, the wizard asks you for any contents you want to appear on certain pages. You're asked to identify standard elements that appear on a group of pages and any information that you want displayed on a particular page. In keeping with the rest of the wizard's user-friendly interface, you specify the contents by selecting or clearing check boxes or option buttons.

Choose a Design for Your Web Site ● NEW FEATURE

Once you've selected the standard page contents for your Web, you have the chance to design your Web as well by clicking the wizard's Choose Web Theme button. The Choose Theme dialog box appears with a full section of design schemes you can apply to some or all of the pages in the Web you're creating. To give the theme you've chosen some extra pizzazz, select the check boxes next to Vivid Colors and Active Graphics. If you want a simple, solid background color instead of a design, clear the Background Picture check box. You can easily review and customize themes later on.

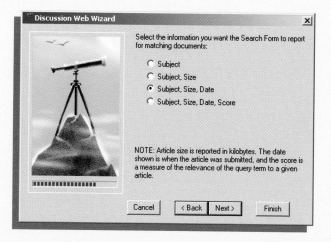

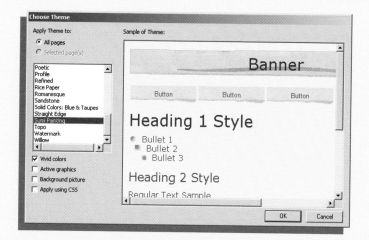

Applying a Theme ❂ NEW FEATURE

FrontPage comes with collections of color and graphic arrangements called *themes* that you can use to give your Web pages a professional look and feel. Themes include colors that complement one another, type fonts that are distinctive, and buttons that you don't have to draw on your own.

Review and Choose a Theme

(1) Open the Web page or Web site to which you want to apply a theme.

(2) Choose Theme from the Format menu.

(3) Select All Pages or Selected Page(s) to apply the theme to all of the current Web's pages, just the current page, or to selected pages.

(4) Click a theme's name to view a preview in the Sample Of Theme box on the right.

(5) Select one or more of the following check boxes to vary the theme's appearance:

- Vivid Colors intensifies the colors displayed by the theme.

- Active Graphics makes the buttons and other graphics stand out.

- Background Picture adds a background design to the theme.

- Apply Using CSS creates the theme using Cascading Style Sheets.

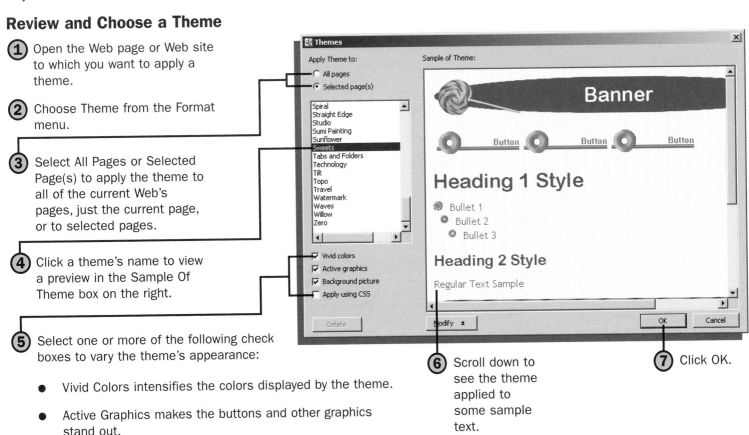

(6) Scroll down to see the theme applied to some sample text.

(7) Click OK.

Customize a Theme

(1) Select a theme, and then click Modify at the bottom of the Themes dialog box to display a new set of buttons.

(3) Choose a color scheme from the selections shown in the Color Schemes tab, or use the Color Wheel and Custom tabs to select your own set of colors, and then click OK.

(2) Click Colors to select a new color scheme.

(4) Click Graphics to customize the graphics in the theme.

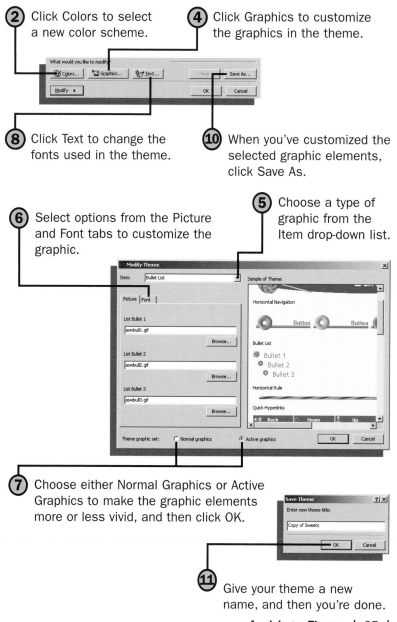

(8) Click Text to change the fonts used in the theme.

(10) When you've customized the selected graphic elements, click Save As.

(6) Select options from the Picture and Font tabs to customize the graphic.

(5) Choose a type of graphic from the Item drop-down list.

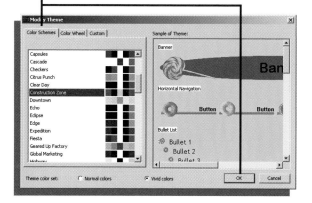

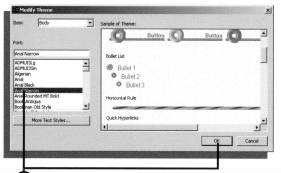

(9) Click a font in the Font box to see it displayed in the sample theme on the right, and then click OK when you're happy with your choice.

(7) Choose either Normal Graphics or Active Graphics to make the graphic elements more or less vivid, and then click OK.

(11) Give your theme a new name, and then you're done.

Saving a FrontPage-based Web

Once you've created your FrontPage-based Web, you need to save your changes. You've got several options for where to save your files. If your Web exists only on your computer, you can save your changes without changing the name or location of the Web. However, you may want to save your Web to another networked computer or to the Web server that will host your pages. FrontPage makes the process of saving and exporting files a seamless operation.

Save to Your Local Computer

① Click the Save button.

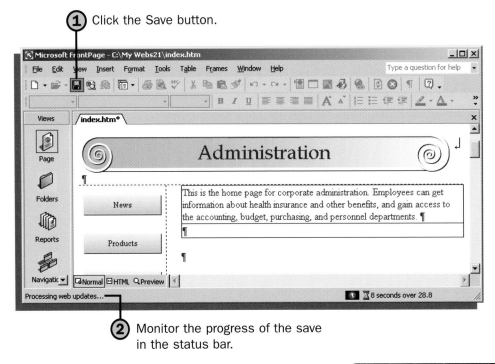

② Monitor the progress of the save in the status bar.

> **! TIP: If you want the current page to serve as a model for other pages, you can save it as a template. Select Save As from the File menu. In the Save As dialog box, select FrontPage Template from the Save As Type drop-down list, and then click Save.**

Save to a New Location

(1) Select one of the following options:

- Choose Save As from the File menu if you only want to save the current Web page.

- Choose Save All from the File menu if you want to save all pages in the current Web.

(2) If you choose Save As, make a selection from the Save In drop-down list to specify the folder where you want to save the Web page, image, or set of pages.

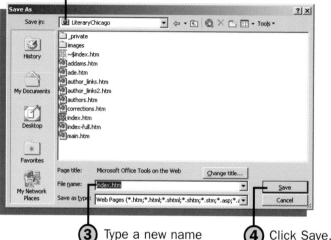

(3) Type a new name in the File Name box, if you wish.

(4) Click Save.

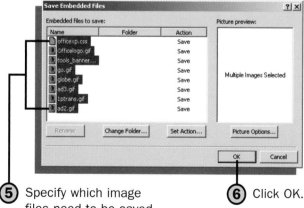

(5) Specify which image files need to be saved with the Web page or pages, and where to save them.

(6) Click OK.

Save to a Web Server

1 On the Windows desktop, open My Network Places, double-click Add Network Place, and then follow the Add Network Place Wizard to create a Web folder.

2 Choosing Save As from the FrontPage File menu brings up the Save As dialog box.

3 Click My Network Places.

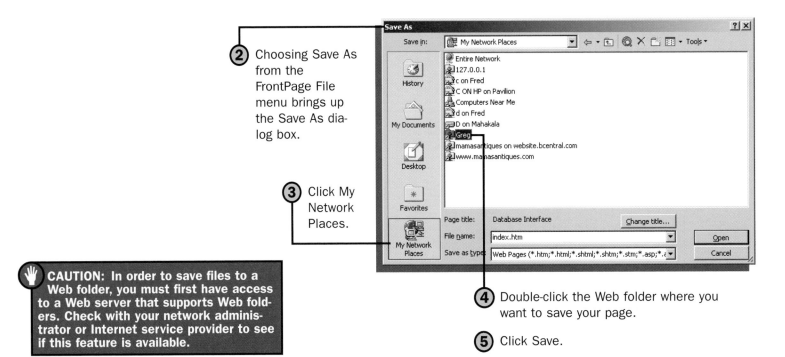

4 Double-click the Web folder where you want to save your page.

5 Click Save.

> ✋ **CAUTION:** In order to save files to a Web folder, you must first have access to a Web server that supports Web folders. Check with your network administrator or Internet service provider to see if this feature is available.

Opening and Closing an Existing Web

After you've got a few Web pages and perhaps even a few FrontPage-based Web sites under your belt, chances are you'll be spending most of your time working with existing Webs rather than creating new ones from scratch. Maintaining and updating a Web site is an important job. FrontPage makes it easy to work with existing Webs, and especially easy to reopen Webs you've worked with recently.

Open a Local Web

(1) Perform one of the following actions:

- Click the down arrow on the Open button, and then choose Open Web from the shortcut menu.

- Choose the name of a Web from the Recent Webs submenu of the File menu.

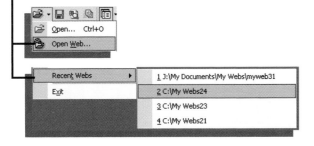

(2) In the Open Web dialog box (which appears if you choose Open Web), specify the Web's location in the Look In drop-down list.

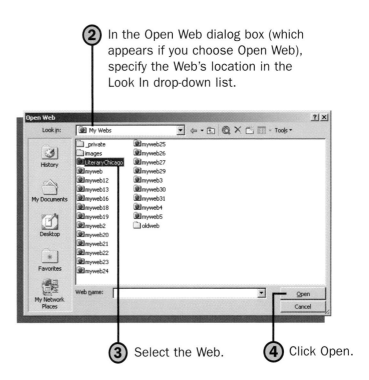

(3) Select the Web.　(4) Click Open.

Open a Web from a Server

(1) Click the down arrow on the Open button, and then choose Open Web from the shortcut menu.

(2) Enter the URL of the Web server you want to access in the Web Name box.

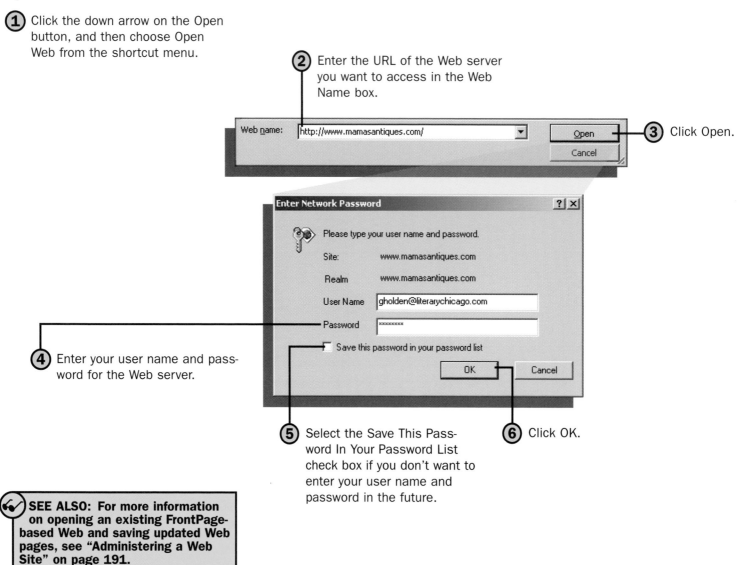

Web name: http://www.mamasantiques.com/   Open   **(3)** Click Open.
                                          Cancel

Enter Network Password   ? X

Please type your user name and password.

Site: www.mamasantiques.com

Realm   www.mamasantiques.com

User Name   gholden@literarychicago.com

Password   ××××××××

☐ Save this password in your password list

         OK   Cancel

(4) Enter your user name and password for the Web server.

(5) Select the Save This Password In Your Password List check box if you don't want to enter your user name and password in the future.

(6) Click OK.

SEE ALSO: For more information on opening an existing FrontPage-based Web and saving updated Web pages, see "Administering a Web Site" on page 191.

Adding Text to a Web Page

NEW FEATURE

Graphics and multimedia might make the Web a feast for the eyes, but text is the bread-and-butter of any Web site. Once you have your site's framework established, you will need to fill your pages with words that attract the attention of your visitors and keep them coming back for more.

Whether you're creating your Web site just for fun or as a source of income, content is your most important product. The best content takes your visitors' needs and tastes into account and gives them information they can really use. Where do you come up with such information? You can type the words from scratch and format them right in the FrontPage window—the FrontPage textual editing tools will be familiar to anyone who has used Word or other word processing software. You can copy text from other Office applications and paste it into your file. You can even insert an entire file or borrow text from another Web page.

In this section, you learn how to add text to your FrontPage-based Web and then edit it into readable, compelling prose. You'll learn how to use FrontPage's built-in spelling checker and thesaurus, format characters and paragraphs, and preview and print your documents.

Entering Web Page Text

When it comes to typing and formatting your words, FrontPage works just like a good word processor. You use the text cursor to enter, select, delete, and cut-and-paste text quickly and easily. If you need to, you can take advantage of the program's new speech recognition capabilities to get your message onto your Web page.

⚠ **TIP:** By default, FrontPage automatically checks your spelling and grammar while you type. Any misspelled words are underlined in red, while grammar errors are underlined in green.

Type Text

⚠ **TIP:** FrontPage automatically converts any e-mail or Web page address that you type into a hyperlink.

① Open the FrontPage-based Web you want to edit.

② Double-click the file name of the Web page you want to work on.

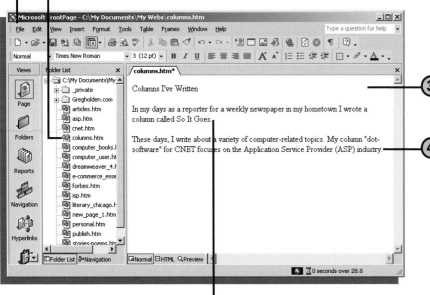

③ Click in the main display area where you want to add text.

④ Type your text, and let FrontPage perform word wrap.

⑤ Press Enter when you want to start a new paragraph.

✓ **SEE ALSO:** You can manually check the spelling or grammar of a document—see page 54 for more information. Also see "Using Navigation Elements" on page 111 for more about hyperlinks.

Use Speech Recognition

(1) Choose Speech from the Tools menu.

(2) Click Microphone on the Language bar if the microphone is not already turned on. If this is the first time you're using Speech Recognition, you will be asked to configure your microphone and to train Office for speech recognition. Otherwise, begin speaking slowly and clearly.

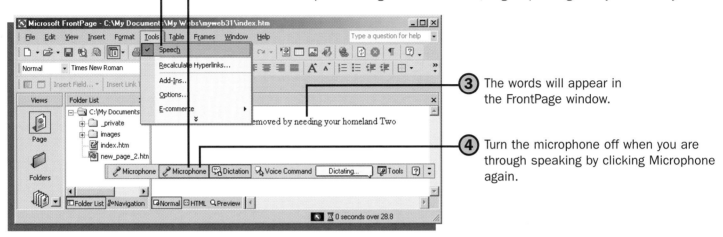

(3) The words will appear in the FrontPage window.

(4) Turn the microphone off when you are through speaking by clicking Microphone again.

> **! TIP:** You may not already have Speech Recognition installed. To install it, log on as Administrator, open the Control Panel, double-click the Add/Remove Programs icon, and then select Microsoft Office XP Standard or Microsoft Office XP Professional (whichever is installed) from the Currently Installed Programs list. Click Change, select Add Or Remove Features, and then in Office Shared Features select Alternative User Input and click Run All From My Computer. Click Update to install speech and handwriting recognition.

> **CAUTION:** Don't expect FrontPage to handle your dictation perfectly the first time around. After you speak your words, check the spelling and edit them. And for best results, use a microphone equipped with gain adjustment, a feature that amplifies your voice so your computer can hear everything you're saying. Also, position your microphone about an inch from your mouth so your voice doesn't become distorted.

Where Do I Get the Text?

Content is king on the Web. Small, quirky sites that are full of cleverly written information can attract more visits than large corporate Web sites that restate bland copy taken from their annual reports. Do some brainstorming and note-taking about what you want to communicate online and exactly who you want to attract.

Readers on the Web are in a hurry. They're used to moving from site to site rapidly. They also want variety. Any well-written Web page contains a variety of content. Think about gathering text that can be divided into headings, body text, lists, and hyperlinks, as shown below.

If You're Creating a Personal Web Site

Stop and think about information you can provide that readers might actually use. Publish your favorite family recipes, or provide recommendations of hotels you've enjoyed or attractions you've discovered while on vacation. If you're involved in political causes or personal issues that have a strong impact on your life, tell people about them and suggest ways they can get involved as well.

If You're Creating a Work-Related Site

Chances are you're awash in a sea of reports, memos, employee handbooks, and the like. Keep two essential things in mind when you're gathering text for a business-related Web: get the right people to sign off with approvals, and give yourself enough time. For a small Web site with perhaps a dozen separate articles, allot three months to get everything done. Also build in time to update your Web site's content on a regular basis.

If You're Starting an Online Business

Many successful e-commerce sites provide content that doesn't directly deal with sales. On Golfballs.com (*www.golfballs.com*), you can read about the history of golf, for instance. The more background information you provide about your products, the more reasons you give shoppers to visit your site regularly, and the stronger the relationship you establish with prospective customers.

Copying and Moving Text to a Web Page

You don't need to create all your text by typing it from scratch. Nor does it have to be in the perfect location the first time you type it. You'll save time—and possibly save yourself some spelling errors—by copying or moving it from one location to another. The processes are exactly the same as in your word processor: you can copy and paste using toolbar buttons, or drag text to move it.

Copy Text Within a Page

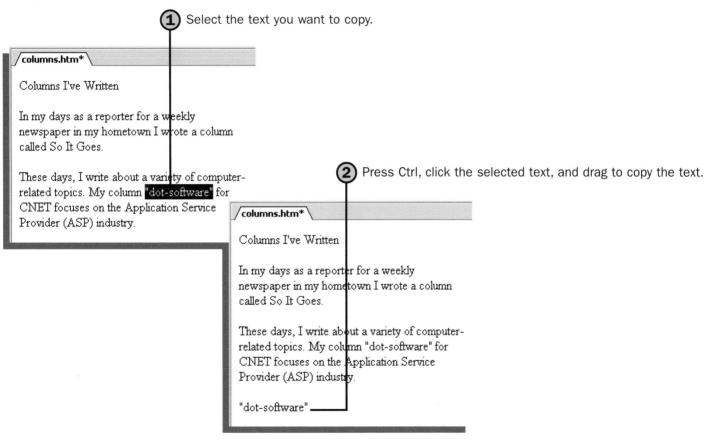

1 Select the text you want to copy.

2 Press Ctrl, click the selected text, and drag to copy the text.

Copy Text Between Pages

(1) Double-click the Folder List icons to open the files you want to work with.

(2) Select the text you want to copy.

(3) Click the Copy button.

First open page

Second open page

(4) Click the tab for the second page.

(5) Position the text cursor in the location where you want to paste the text.

(6) Click the Paste button.

(7) A Paste Options icon appears. If you don't want to keep the formatting of the text (in this case, the hyperlink), click the Paste Options icon down arrow and then select Keep Text Only.

Paste Options icon

TIP: You can use the same sorts of short-cuts for selecting text that you've probably used in your word processor: double-click the word to select it; triple-click anywhere in a paragraph to select it; or click and drag your text cursor across text to select it.

TRY THIS: If you want to copy text from one window and paste it into another one, here's a shortcut: Open two or more FrontPage files at the same time, and then click the FrontPage Window menu. Switch between the windows by selecting their names from the Window menu.

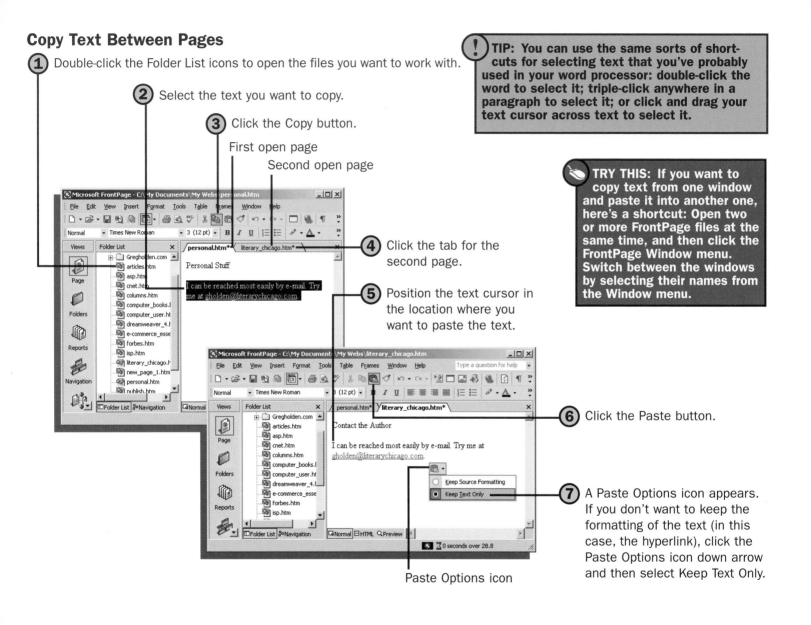

Move Text Within a Page

(1) Select the text you want to move.

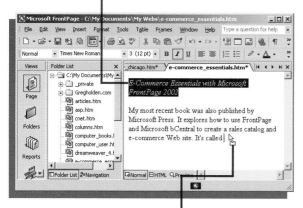

(2) Click the selected text, hold down your mouse button, and drag it to the new location. As you drag, the text cursor will become an arrow and a gray text cursor will mark where the text will appear.

(3) Release your mouse button to drop the text into the new location.

Drag-and-Drop Between Pages

(1) Open the origin and destination pages, and arrange both so you can see them on your screen.

(2) Select the text you want to copy in the first page.

(3) Click the selected text, hold down the mouse button, and drag it to the desired location in the second page.

Using the Office Clipboard ⊙ NEW FEATURE

Chances are you've got a wealth of text that you can copy and paste into your FrontPage-based Web. If you work in an office, you've probably got newsletters, manuals, and other textual sources. You can use the Office Clipboard to keep track of what you want to copy into FrontPage.

The Office Clipboard is a part of your computer memory that serves as a holding area for text or other objects you want to move from one location to another: When you choose Cut or Copy from an Office application's Edit menu, what you've selected goes into the Clipboard. You can then paste it somewhere else.

Suppose you want to copy two paragraphs from an office handbook into a Web page, and the paragraphs are in different locations in the same Word document. Copy the two chunks of text, one after another, and then switch to FrontPage. Choose Office Clipboard from the FrontPage Edit menu, and the contents of the clipboard are displayed in the Clipboard task pane. As the following figure shows, you can use the task pane to paste the Clipboard's contents or perform other tasks.

The Options menu at the bottom of the Office Clipboard task pane lets you control when you want the Clipboard to appear and how you want it to operate.

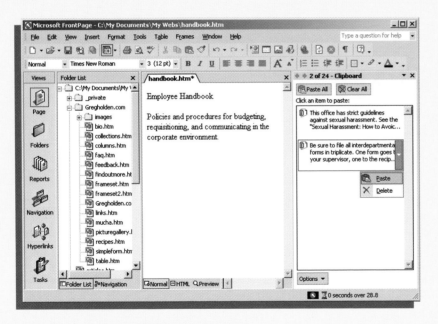

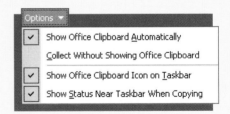

Editing Web Page Text

FrontPage isn't just a powerful Web site editor. It's a powerful word processing tool as well. Take a few minutes to familiarize yourself with the shortcuts and tools the program gives you for selecting and editing your text. Over the course of a long document you can save a substantial amount of time.

Undo a Mistake

(1) If you want to undo the last text entry or edit you performed, click the Undo button.

(2) To undo a series of actions, click the Undo button down arrow and select the actions from the list. Microsoft FrontPage maintains a list of the last 30 actions and lets you undo each in sequence.

Redo a Task

(1) If you have undone the pasting or typing of text, or some other action that you want to redo, click the Redo button.

(2) To redo multiple actions, click the Redo button down arrow and choose from the list of recent actions. Microsoft FrontPage maintains a list of the last 30 actions and lets you redo each.

Delete Text

(1) Scroll across the text you want to delete.

(2) Press the Cut button.

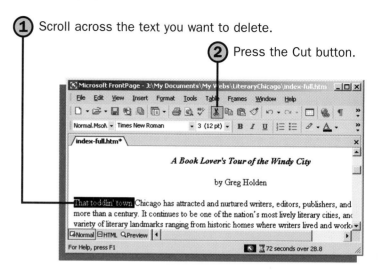

> **! TIP:** You'll have an easier time editing your document if you clear away the Folder List and Views bar so you can see more of your page. Choose each one in turn from the Views menu to hide them.

> **! TIP:** The Redo button is only active after you have used the Undo button.

Using Text from Other Documents

There's no need to re-create text files that you or others have already created and that you want to add to your Web site. If you have a word processing file that you're happy with and want to publish in its entirety, you can insert the entire file. Other times, you might want to copy text from another Web page into the Web site you're assembling. Here, too, Microsoft FrontPage allows you to copy text from a file while keeping the original document's formatting.

Insert a File

1 Open the Web page into which you want to insert the file, and then click to position the cursor at the place where you want to add the text.

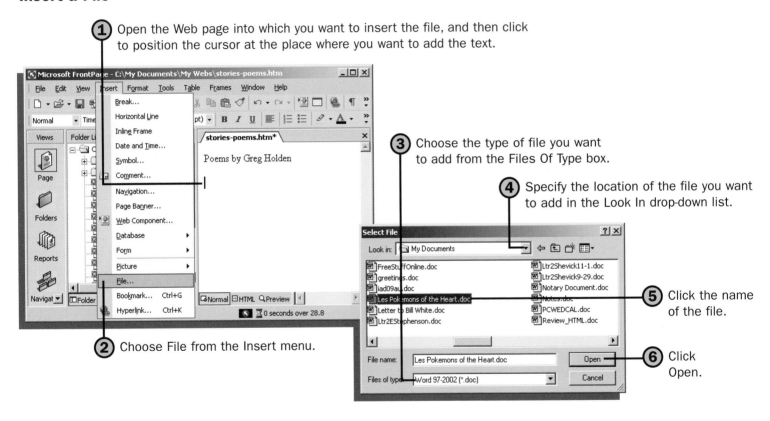

2 Choose File from the Insert menu.

3 Choose the type of file you want to add from the Files Of Type box.

4 Specify the location of the file you want to add in the Look In drop-down list.

5 Click the name of the file.

6 Click Open.

Copy Text from Another File

① Open a Word document or other word processing file.

② Select the text you want to copy.

③ Click the Copy button.

④ Click to position the cursor at the location in your Web page where you want the text to appear.

⑤ Click the Paste button.

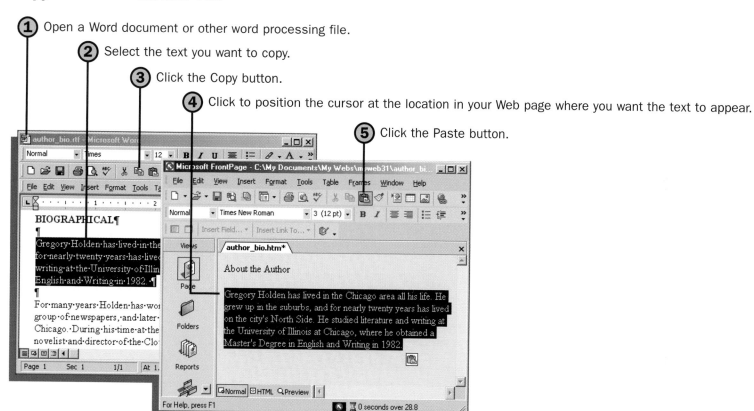

> **! TIP:** If you don't have toolbars showing in your word processing file, press Ctrl+C to copy selected text. You can then press Ctrl+V to paste it.

Checking Your Spelling and Word Choice

Errors in a Web page detract from your site's message. If you're in business, this can cost you money. Luckily, FrontPage gives you access to the same powerful spelling checker and grammar utilities used by other Office applications. If you're in a hurry, you can let FrontPage check your spelling and grammar as you type. You can also manually check your spelling one page at a time or an entire FrontPage-based Web.

Check Spelling Within a Page

(1) Click Page on the Views bar.

(2) Click the Spelling button.

! TIP: To turn automatic spelling checking on or off, choose Page Options from the Tools menu. Click General, and either select or clear the Check Spelling As You Type box.

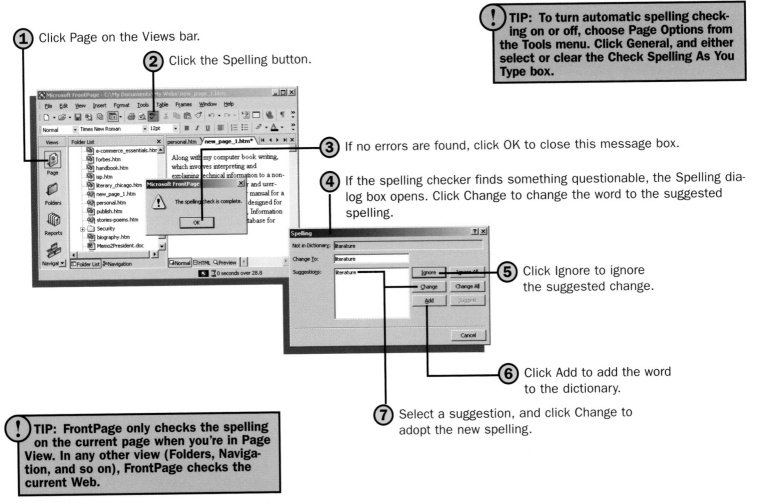

(3) If no errors are found, click OK to close this message box.

(4) If the spelling checker finds something questionable, the Spelling dialog box opens. Click Change to change the word to the suggested spelling.

(5) Click Ignore to ignore the suggested change.

(6) Click Add to add the word to the dictionary.

(7) Select a suggestion, and click Change to adopt the new spelling.

! TIP: FrontPage only checks the spelling on the current page when you're in Page View. In any other view (Folders, Navigation, and so on), FrontPage checks the current Web.

Use the Thesaurus

① Select the word for which you're seeking a synonym.

② Choose Thesaurus from the Tools menu.

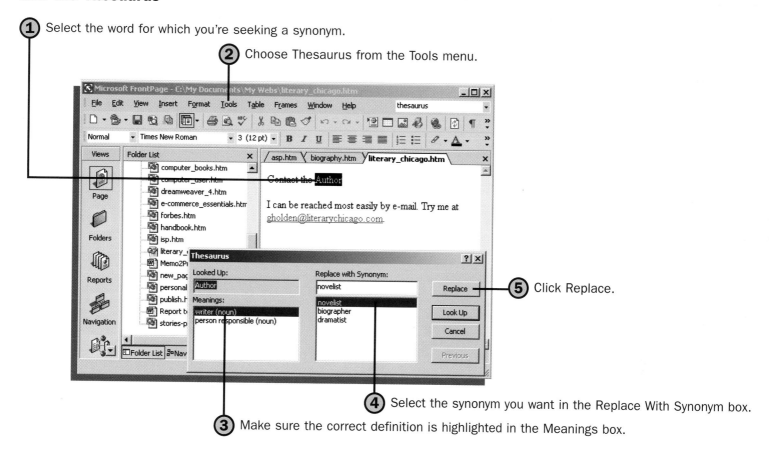

⑤ Click Replace.

④ Select the synonym you want in the Replace With Synonym box.

③ Make sure the correct definition is highlighted in the Meanings box.

> **TIP: Click Look Up to search for the definition of any word that's displayed in the Replace With Synonym area of the Thesaurus dialog box.**

Formatting Characters

Web surfers need all the help they can get to read text on their computer screens. Large chunks of text are hard to read when they're all in the same size, typeface, and style. You can give your words the impact they need by choosing styles and fonts from the FrontPage toolbars and menus.

Choose a Font

(1) Select the text you want to format.

(2) Click the Font drop-down list.

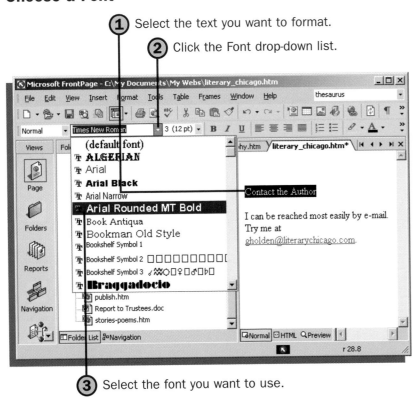

(3) Select the font you want to use.

Assign Text Styles

(1) Select the text you want to format.

(2) Click the Bold, Italic, or Underline button in the Formatting toolbar.

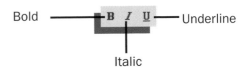

Bold — **B** *I* <u>U</u> — Underline

Italic

> **CAUTION: Because hyperlinks are commonly underlined on Web pages, you should use underlining sparingly. Your readers might mistake underlined text for a link.**

> **CAUTION: Before you choose an exotic-looking font you have on your system, you need to realize that visitors to your site won't see the font unless they, too, have it installed on their computers. To be safe, choose the default font or common ones such as Arial, Helvetica, Times, or Verdana.**

Add Color to Text

(1) Select the text you want to format.

TIP: Click the Highlight Color button down arrow if you want to highlight the space around the letters as well as the letters themselves.

(2) Click the Font Color button down arrow to change the color of the letters.

(3) Click the square that represents the color you want.

(4) Click More Colors if you want to choose a different color.

(5) In the More Colors dialog box, choose one of the color hexagons to select it.

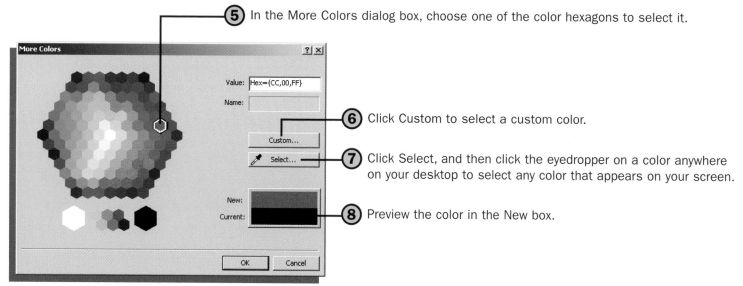

(6) Click Custom to select a custom color.

(7) Click Select, and then click the eyedropper on a color anywhere on your desktop to select any color that appears on your screen.

(8) Preview the color in the New box.

TRY THIS: Choose Font from the Format menu to change the selected text's size and font or add attributes you can't find on the toolbars, such as small caps, all caps, and other unusual styles. You also get a preview of the attributes you've chosen so you can see how the font will look before you make the changes.

Changing Text Size

By making some text larger and some text smaller on your FrontPage-based Web pages, you indicate which contents you want your visitors to look at first. To call attention to text you want to emphasize, you can change the font size or you can create headings and subheadings. Headings control the size of text by assigning a heading style to text rather than a point size. Heading 1 is the largest; Heading 6 is the smallest. The viewer's browser will determine what size to use when displaying headings.

Specify a Text Size

1 Select the text you want to format.

2 Click the Font Size drop-down list, and choose a size.

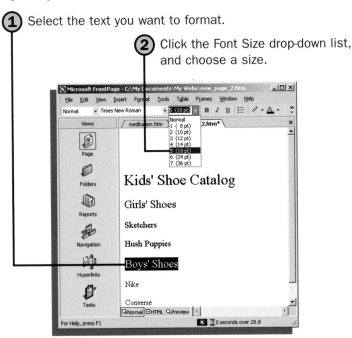

Create a Heading

1 Type the text that you want to turn into a heading.

2 Select the heading text.

3 Click the Style drop-down list.

4 Choose the heading style you want.

! TIP: You can express font size on a Web page in two ways: as a specific point value (approximately 72 points to an inch) or a relative value (1, 2, 3, 4, 5, 6, and 7).

Create a Subheading

1 After you type the text beneath the main heading, press Enter to start a new paragraph.

2 Type and select the subheading text.

3 Click the Style drop-down list.

4 Select the subheading style you want.

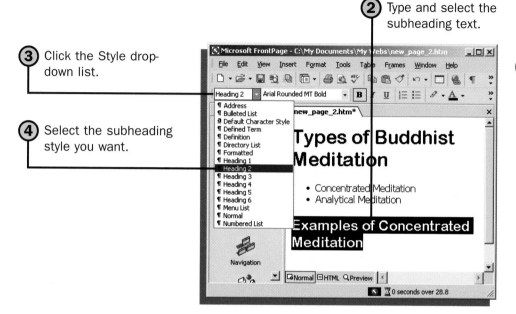

TIP: Sometimes, if the FrontPage window you're working in is too narrow, the Font Size drop-down list won't appear. Drag the right edge of the window to the right to enlarge it until the Font Size drop-down list appears.

TIP: Readers on the Web are usually in a hurry, so don't get too creative with headings; use Heading 1 for the main heading on a page, Heading 2 for the second-most-important heading, and so on. Don't place larger size headings lower on the page than smaller ones.

CAUTION: Remember that your words are going to be read on a computer screen. Don't make body text so small that people have to squint and strain to read it. A reliable size for body text is 12 pt. (or, if you use relative font sizes, 3). The smallest heading sizes, Heading 5 and Heading 6, are rarely used because they're hard to read.

Formatting Paragraphs

The paragraph is the fundamental unit you need to work with when designing your Web pages. Paragraphs are easy to create in FrontPage: when you press Enter, FrontPage skips a line so you can begin a new paragraph. FrontPage also lets you perform a full range of paragraph-level formatting tasks. You can indent, align, or control the spacing of paragraphs.

Choose Alignment

① Click anywhere in the paragraph you want to align.

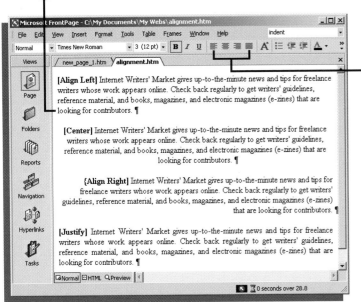

② Click one of the following buttons:

- Align Left to align the left side of the paragraph flush with the left margin.

- Align Right to align the right side of the paragraph flush with the right margin.

- Center to center each line horizontally.

- Justify to align both the right and left sides of the paragraph flush with the right and left margins.

TRY THIS: To control the right-hand margin of a paragraph, insert one or more line breaks. Click within the paragraph to position the text cursor. Then hold down the Shift key while pressing Enter to break the line without starting a new paragraph.

TIP: When you're aligning or indenting paragraphs, you don't have to select the entire paragraph to format it. You only need to position the text cursor anywhere within the paragraph or select a word or phrase within it.

Fine-Tune Indentation and Control Spacing

(1) Select one or more paragraphs you want to format.

(2) Right-click on a paragraph, and select Paragraph from the shortcut menu.

(3) To indent the left margin of the paragraph, either click the Before Text up arrow to specify a value in pixels or type the value into the box.

(5) To indent the right margin of the paragraph, either click the After Text up arrow to specify a value or type the value into the box.

(6) Preview the indentation in the Preview box.

(4) To indent only the first line, either click the Indent First Line up arrow to specify a value in pixels or type the value into the box.

(7) Click the Before up arrow or type the value into the box, to increase spacing (in pixels) between the paragraph you are formatting and the previous paragraph.

(8) Click the After up arrow or type the value into the box, to increase spacing between the paragraph you are formatting and the following paragraph.

(10) Click OK.

(9) Choose an option from the Line Spacing drop-down list to change the space between lines.

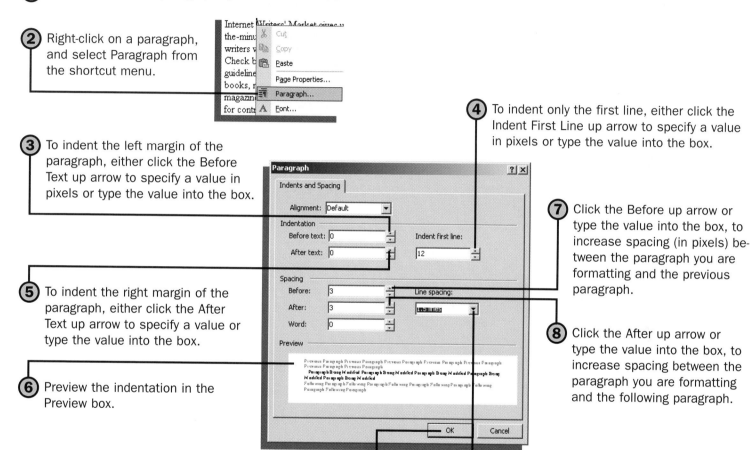

Working with Bulleted and Numbered Lists

Lists provide you with a great way to present information on any Web page. They break up Web page text and make contents much more readable. A bulleted list shows a group of separate items that don't have a specific order. A numbered list, on the other hand, is perfect for leading your readers through a series of steps they need to follow in order (such as the steps you see throughout this book). FrontPage makes it simple for you turn a group of paragraphs into a list. You can then customize the list to change the number or bullet style.

Turn a Group of Paragraphs into a Bulleted List

1. Type a series of list items. After each item, press Enter to start a new paragraph.

2. Select all of the list items you want to format.

3. Click the Bullets button.

Change Bullet Style

1. Select the bulleted list items you want to format.

2. Choose Bullets And Numbering from the Format menu.

3. Click the Plain Bullets tab.

4. Click the picture that represents the style of bullet you want.

5. Click OK.

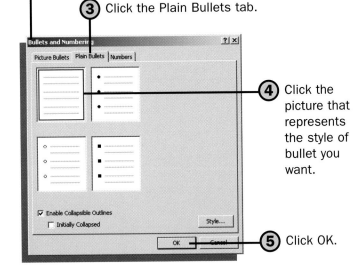

Turn Paragraphs into a Numbered List

(1) Type a series of steps, in order. Press Enter after each one to start a new paragraph.

(3) Click the Numbering button.

(2) Select the set of paragraphs that you want to convert.

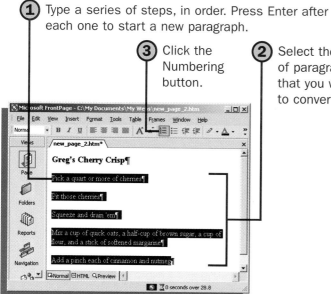

Change Number Style

(1) Select the set of list items you want to format.

(2) Choose Bullets And Numbering from the Format menu.

(3) Click the Numbers tab.

(4) Click the picture that represents the style of numbers you want.

(5) Type a number in the Start At box if you want the list to start at a number other than 1 or a letter other than A.

(6) Click OK.

TRY THIS: To create a two-line definition, type the term to be defined on one line, press Enter, and then type the definition on the next line. Click anywhere in the first line, and then choose Defined Term from the Style drop-down list. Click anywhere in the second line, and then choose Definition from the Style drop-down list. You've just created the third type of Web page list—a definition list.

CAUTION: When you create a numbered list, don't type the numbers yourself. If you do, when you click Numbering, you'll end up with two sets of numbers before each list item.

Adding Horizontal Lines

When you organize your Web pages by distinguishing one section from another, you make your contents easier to read. One of the most effective ways to separate sections of a Web page is by adding a horizontal line. You can customize the line by making it a solid color or changing its thickness or width.

Break Text with Lines

1 Press Enter to insert a blank paragraph at the spot where you want to divide two sections of your Web page.

2 Choose Horizontal Line from the Insert menu.

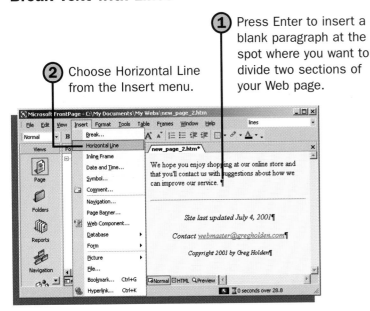

Customize a Line's Appearance

1 Right-click the horizontal line you want to customize.

2 Choose Horizontal Line Properties from the shortcut menu.

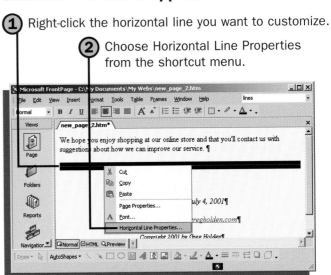

! **TIP:** You can cut and paste a horizontal line just as you would with text. Select the line by clicking on it once to highlight it, then click the Cut button, reposition the cursor, and click the Paste button to insert the line.

SEE ALSO: If a theme has been applied to the page you are working on, the horizontal line you add might be in a color or have a stylized appearance. For more information, see "Applying a Theme" on page 34.

TRY THIS: You can use an image as a horizontal line. Click to position the cursor at the insertion point. Select Clip Art from the Picture submenu of the Insert menu, search for "line," and select the clip art line image by clicking on it.

TIP: If you add a horizontal line to a page that has a theme applied, you can only change the alignment of the line. You can't change its color or thickness.

3 Enter a value for the width of the line, either in pixels or as a percentage of page width in the Width box.

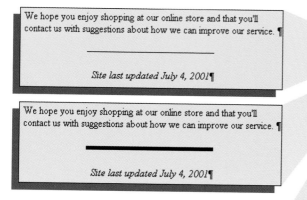

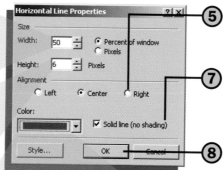

5 In the Alignment area, specify the desired alignment of a line whose width you've already shortened.

7 Select the Solid Line (No Shading) check box if you want a solid black line rather than one with a shadow.

8 Click OK.

4 Specify the height (or thickness) of the line in the Height box.

6 Select a color for the line from the Color drop-down list.

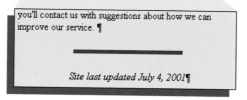

CAUTION: If you specify a width in pixels for a horizontal line, your viewer might undo your work by resizing the browser window. If you've specified that the line should be 300 pixels and the viewer resizes the browser window to, say 275 or 300 pixels, the line will seem to cover the entire width of the window. Use percentages to take window size into account.

Finding and Replacing Text

Web sites can contain many separate documents contained in different folders, and making a change to text that recurs in many of those pages can be a tedious process—unless you use the FrontPage ability to find and replace text. This feature is effective for making changes quickly to all the pages in a Web site. FrontPage also has a Search function that enables you to locate text, files, or other Web site contents.

Find Text

(1) Open the FrontPage-based Web you want to search.

(2) Choose Find from the Edit menu to open the Find And Replace dialog box.

(3) Type the text you want to search for in the Find What box.

(4) Specify where you want FrontPage to look by clicking one of the buttons in the Find Where area.

(5) Select the Match Case check box if you want to match the case of the Find What text exactly.

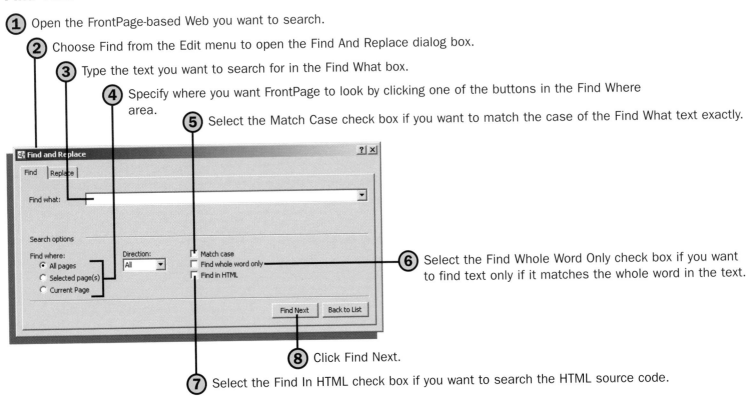

(6) Select the Find Whole Word Only check box if you want to find text only if it matches the whole word in the text.

(8) Click Find Next.

(7) Select the Find In HTML check box if you want to search the HTML source code.

Replace Text

(1) Choose Replace from the Edit menu, or click the Replace tab if the Find And Replace dialog box is already open.

(2) If necessary, enter the text you want to look for in the Find What box.

(3) Enter the replacement text in the Replace With box.

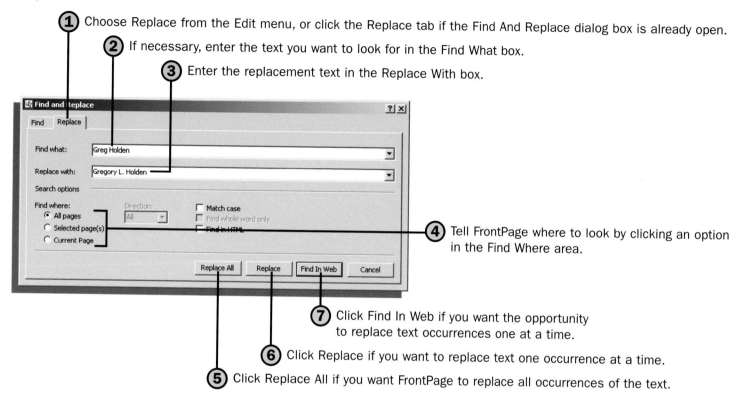

(4) Tell FrontPage where to look by clicking an option in the Find Where area.

(7) Click Find In Web if you want the opportunity to replace text occurrences one at a time.

(6) Click Replace if you want to replace text one occurrence at a time.

(5) Click Replace All if you want FrontPage to replace all occurrences of the text.

Printing and Previewing Pages

The Web pages you create are intended to be viewed on a computer monitor rather than on paper. However, it's sometimes useful to print out pages so you can work on them outside the office or show them to other people. FrontPage gives you a chance to look at the page as it will appear when you print it.

Preview a Page

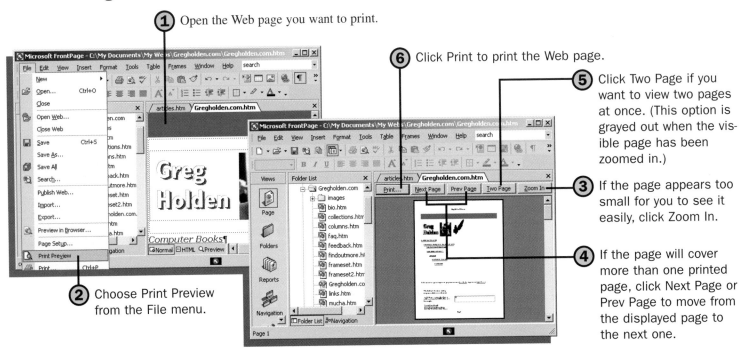

① Open the Web page you want to print.

⑥ Click Print to print the Web page.

⑤ Click Two Page if you want to view two pages at once. (This option is grayed out when the visible page has been zoomed in.)

③ If the page appears too small for you to see it easily, click Zoom In.

④ If the page will cover more than one printed page, click Next Page or Prev Page to move from the displayed page to the next one.

② Choose Print Preview from the File menu.

 CAUTION: You can't make changes to a Web page in Print Preview, even when you zoom in on its contents. You need to switch back to Page view by closing the Print Preview display and then reopening the page so you can make changes.

Print a Page

① Open the Web page you want to prepare for printing, and then click Print on the File menu.

② Select the printer you want to use.

③ Specify the page range you want to print, or click All.

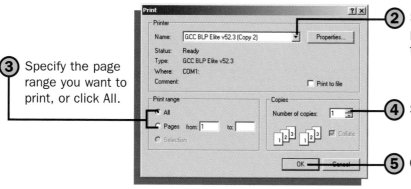

④ Specify the number of copies you want to print.

⑤ Click OK to print the file.

Change Print Options

① Choose Print from the File menu to open the Print dialog box, and then click Properties.

② Specify Portrait or Landscape orientation in the Layout tab.

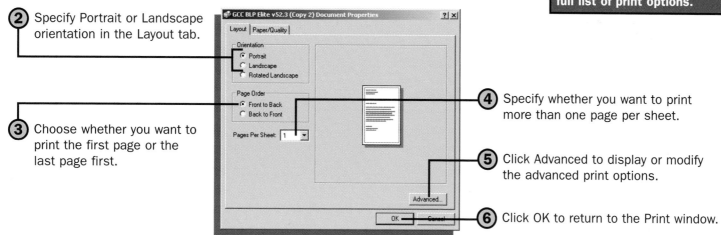

③ Choose whether you want to print the first page or the last page first.

④ Specify whether you want to print more than one page per sheet.

⑤ Click Advanced to display or modify the advanced print options.

⑥ Click OK to return to the Print window.

Adding Images, Sound, and Video

Once you've got your FrontPage-based Web's textual component nailed down, you can enhance your words and make your Web eye-catching and attention-getting by adding images and multimedia.

Working with photos and other images is where a Web page editor really comes in handy. Rather than having to make references to files in HTML, you can see the image as soon as you add it to a Web page. FrontPage makes it easy to adjust the size and appearance of images. You can adjust the space between images and adjacent text with a great deal of precision. You can easily add clickable areas, called *hotspots*, to images, or give images transparent backgrounds, as you'll discover in the following pages.

In this section, you learn about FrontPage's many tools for adding and adjusting graphics, sound, and video files. These include the Pictures toolbar, Image Properties dialog box, Drawing toolbar, and the FrontPage window, which help you turn a simple Web page into a multi-media event with a few mouse clicks.

Inserting Images

Using FrontPage's Insert menu, you can locate an image on your computer or on a networked machine. You can then add the image to a Web page with a single click on the Insert button. Images in FrontPage-based Webs need to be saved in a special format that compresses files so they can be transported and displayed across a network. The two most widely used formats are graphics interchange format (GIF) and Joint Photographic Experts Group (JPG or JPEG).

Add a GIF or JPEG Image

(1) Open the file you want to work with, and click to position the cursor where you want to add the new image.

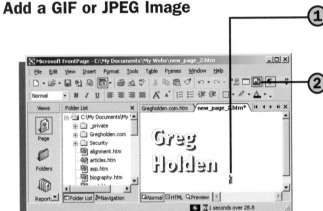

(2) Click the Insert Picture From File button on the Standard toolbar.

> **! TIP:** You can add an image from the World Wide Web by entering its URL in the Picture dialog box.

> **✋ CAUTION:** Web browsers only display GIF, JPG, or PNG images. If you want to add an image in a different file format, you need to convert it to GIF or JPEG, using the procedures described.

(3) Locate the folder that contains the file you want to add.

> **✓ SEE ALSO:** FrontPage works with a wide variety of image formats, including the ones that are especially designed for Web browsers—GIF, JPEG, and Portable Network Graphics (PNG). However, FrontPage is also able to display many other computer image formats, such as Windows bitmap (BMP), Encapsulated PostScript (EPS), tagged image file format (TIF), and Windows Metafile Format (WMF). This enables you to insert a clip art or other image in a non-Web format such as WMF. You can then save the image file in a format that can be displayed on the Web, as explained in "Convert a File to GIF or JPEG" on page 78.

(4) Click the name of the image you want to add.

(5) Click Insert.

Add a Clip Art Image

(1) Click to position the cursor at the location where you want the image to appear.

(2) Choose Clip Art from the Picture submenu of the Insert menu.

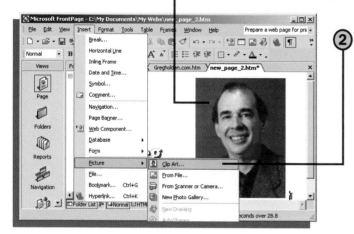

(!) **TIP: Narrowing your search criteria can help you find what you want more quickly. In the Other Search Options area of the Insert Clip Art task pane, click the Search In down arrow to specify a place to search. Click the Results Should Be down arrow to specify a type of image, such as a photo.**

(3) In the task pane, insert a keyword that describes the type of clip art image you want to find.

(4) Click Search.

(5) Click the Forward or the Back button to browse through images found in the Insert Clip Art task pane.

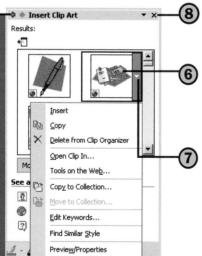

(8) Click the Close button to close the task pane.

(6) Click an image to insert it.

(7) Click the down arrow next to an image to display a shortcut menu with other options.

Searching for the Image You Need

The task pane is only big enough to present a few clip art images at any one time. You can view more images at once and organize your images into collections by using the Clip Organizer, a tool available to FrontPage as well as other Office applications. By clicking a link in the task pane you can be connected instantly to Design Gallery Live, an extensive collection of images that Microsoft makes available to you on the Web. If you can't find what you're looking for on your own computer, you're sure to find it on line.

Use the Clip Organizer

(1) Choose Clip Art from the Picture submenu of the Insert menu.

(2) Scroll to the bottom of the task pane and click Clip Organizer.

(3) Click Collection List to view a list of clip art collections by category.

(4) Scroll down to Office Collections and click the plus sign to view subcategories.

(5) Select a category to see available images.

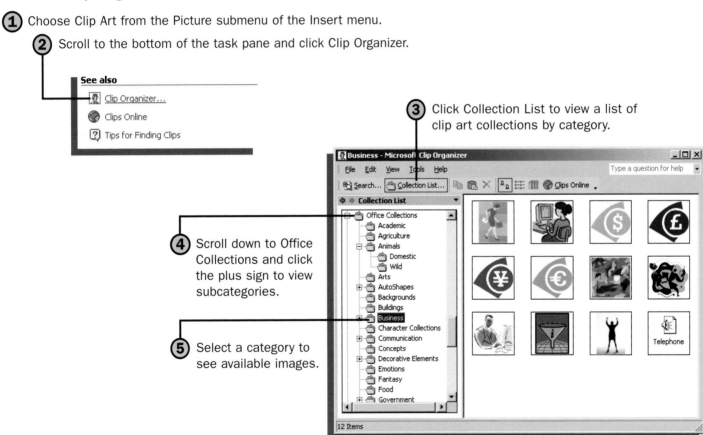

Create a Collection

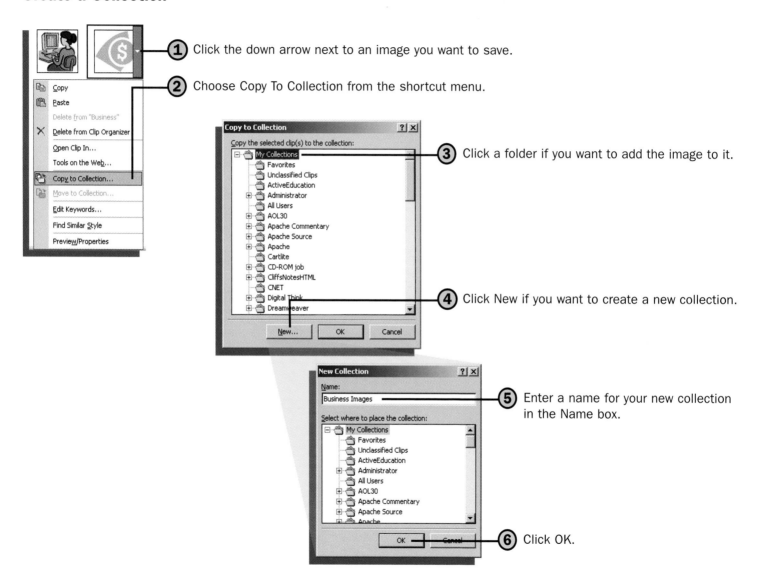

(1) Click the down arrow next to an image you want to save.

(2) Choose Copy To Collection from the shortcut menu.

(3) Click a folder if you want to add the image to it.

(4) Click New if you want to create a new collection.

(5) Enter a name for your new collection in the Name box.

(6) Click OK.

Search for Clips On Line

(1) Open the task pane and click Clip Organizer.

(2) If you can't find what you want in the Clip Organizer, click the Clips Online button. (You must connect to the Internet to perform this option.)

(3) When you connect to the Microsoft Office Design Gallery Live site, read the User License Agreement and click Accept.

(4) Enter a keyword that describes the type of picture you want to locate.

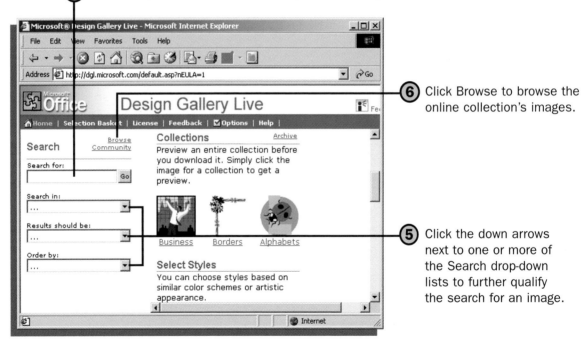

(6) Click Browse to browse the online collection's images.

(5) Click the down arrows next to one or more of the Search drop-down lists to further qualify the search for an image.

TIP: If you don't want to search for clip art based on a keyword and would rather browse all files, click Search on the Clip Organizer toolbar, enter a blank space in the Search Text box, and click Search. The Clip Organizer will browse through all of the Office clip art files and present them for you. This can take a while, but you can save some time by limiting your search to a specific type of file by selecting an option from the Results Should Be drop-down list.

CAUTION: Clip art images are available from other sites around the Web, but read the fine print before you start copying and pasting images. The creators of the images often request that you give them credit, and some of them prohibit commercial use of their images.

TIP: Click Tips For Finding Clips at the bottom of the Insert Clip Art task pane to open FrontPage Help to read suggestions for finding exactly the kind of image you're looking for.

Using Images Wisely

Graphic images are important to getting your message across, but it's easy to defeat the purpose of your page and turn away visitors by overusing images or including images that are too big in file size.

Consider a Web page that consists of a single text file and six images. Chances are the text file is small in size, taking up no more than 5K (kilobytes) of disk space. But if each image is 5K to 10K in size, the total page size easily grows beyond a total of 50K, which can take more than 14 seconds to appear using a 28.8 Kbps modem. To avoid turning away the viewers you're trying to attract, keep the following in mind:

Avoid image overload. Too many Web pages contain four, five, or more images, which have to be downloaded individually. Try to use only one or two images per page.

Monitor download times. Check the download time in the lower right corner of the FrontPage status bar. Choose a relatively slow modem speed such as 28 Kbps (kilobits per second) or 56 Kbps—few of your users will have Internet connections faster than these.

Test your pages. Images appear differently when displayed by different monitors, computers, and browsers. Check your site on as many different types of hardware and software setups as possible.

Edit your images. Web images need to be treated differently than those in print. Crop and resize Web images so they don't take up too much Web page space.

Changing Image File Formats

Different graphics compression formats handle the information in a computer image in different ways. GIF is best suited for line art drawings, while JPEG's method of compression keeps photographs to a small file size while preserving quality. FrontPage gives you access to a far wider range of images than just GIFs or JPEGs. However, to make those images appear on line, you need to convert them to GIF or JPEG format. FrontPage makes this conversion a snap.

Convert a File to GIF or JPEG

(1) Make sure you are in Page View.

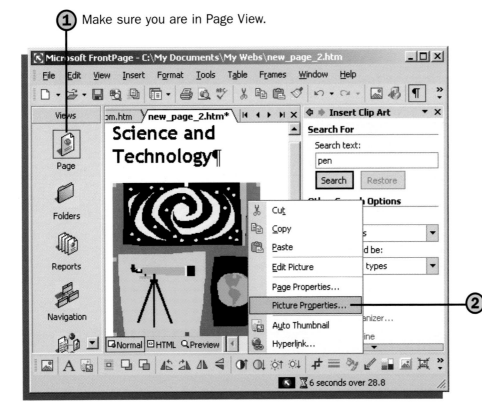

(2) Right-click the image in your page that you want to convert, and then choose Picture Properties from the shortcut menu.

SEE ALSO: You can also switch from another format (such as BMP) to GIF or JPEG in an image editing program such as Microsoft PhotoDraw or Paint Shop Pro. For more information on configuring FrontPage to automatically launch an image editor, see "Customizing FrontPage's Toolbars" on page 220.

3 Click the General tab.

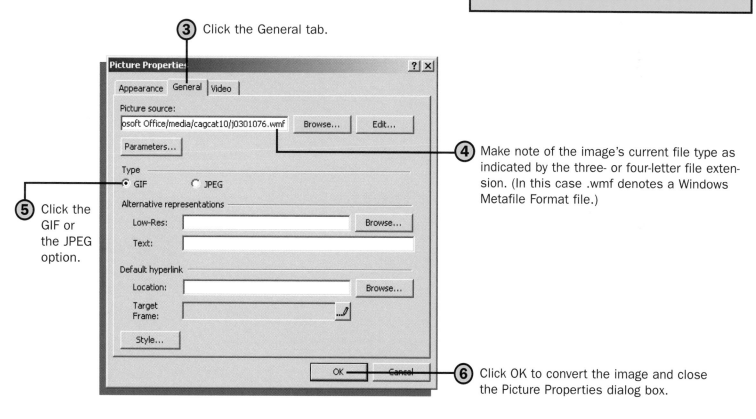

4 Make note of the image's current file type as indicated by the three- or four-letter file extension. (In this case .wmf denotes a Windows Metafile Format file.)

5 Click the GIF or the JPEG option.

6 Click OK to convert the image and close the Picture Properties dialog box.

Copying and Moving Images

FrontPage handles images like other Web page objects, which means it's easy for you to select, copy, and move them. You can move them from one location to another on a page, move them from one page to another, or copy them from a page on the Internet and paste them into the Web site you're working on.

Copy an Image on the Current Page

① Click the image in your page to display the selection handles around it.

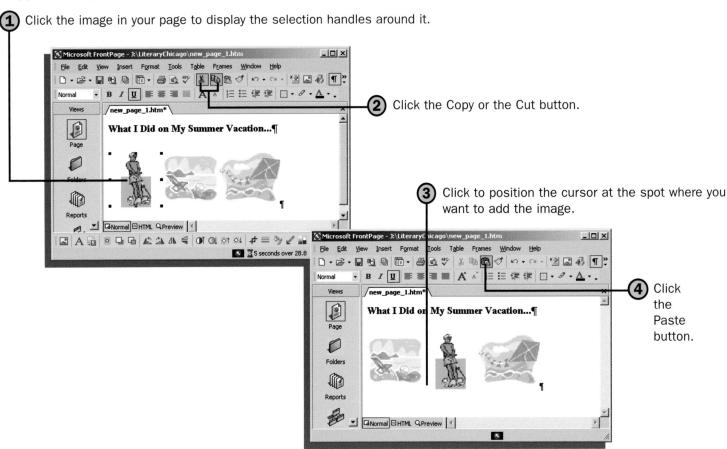

② Click the Copy or the Cut button.

③ Click to position the cursor at the spot where you want to add the image.

④ Click the Paste button.

Move an Image from a Web Page

(1) Open the Web page that contains the image you want to copy.

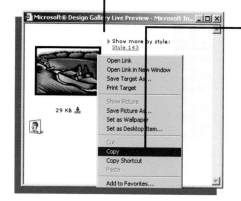

(2) Do one of the following:

- If you're using Microsoft Internet Explorer, right-click the image and choose Copy from the shortcut menu.

- If you're using Netscape Navigator, right-click the image and choose Copy Image Location from the shortcut menu.

(3) Switch back to FrontPage, and click to position the cursor where you want to paste the image.

Paste Button

(4) Do one of the following:

- If you're using Internet Explorer, click the Paste button.

- If you're using Netscape Navigator, click From File on the Picture submenu of the Insert menu, and then paste the image location in the File Name box by pressing Ctrl+V.

CAUTION: Don't copy an image from someone else's Web page unless you have permission from the page's owner to do so.

SEE ALSO: You can also drag-and-drop an image; the steps are the same as with dragging-and-dropping text or other objects. For more information, see "Copying and Moving Text to a Web Page" on page 47.

Cropping and Resizing an Image

It's especially important to control the size of Web page images so they display quickly in a browser window and don't interfere with surrounding text. Two of the easiest ways to adjust image size are cropping (cutting out unnecessary parts of the image) and resizing (making the image smaller in both height and width). While you might prefer to do your cropping and resizing in an image editing program so you have additional control, you can use FrontPage's Pictures toolbar to make the changes without having to switch back and forth between programs.

Crop an Image

1 Click the image in your page to select it. Selection handles tell you the image has been selected.

2 Click the Crop button on the Pictures toolbar. A dashed box will appear.

3 Click one of the handles of the dashed box and drag it inward toward the image to crop it.

4 Click another handle to drag the box around the area of the photo that you want to keep.

5 Click the Crop button again to crop the image.

Resize an Image

① Click the image in your page to select it.

② Click one of the corners of the image, hold down the mouse button, and drag the corner. Drag in toward the center to reduce the image size; drag out to increase the size.

TIP: You can make the Pictures toolbar appear any time by selecting it from the Toolbars submenu of the View menu.

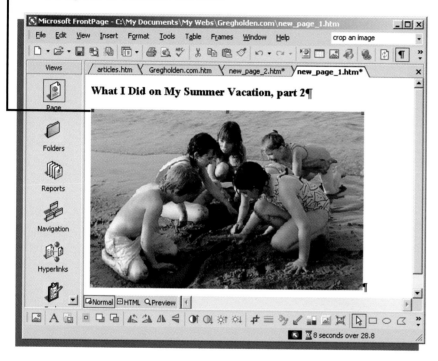

CAUTION: If you clear the Keep Aspect Ratio check box on the Appearance tab of the Picture Properties dialog box and resize a photo, it will become distorted. For instance, if you start with an image that's 500 pixels high and 800 wide and you change the height to 800 without changing the width, the contents of the image will appear to be stretched so they're unnaturally high. To avoid such distortion you need to resize both the height and width at the same ratio, which is what selecting the Keep Aspect Ratio option accomplishes.

TIP: If you change the size of a photo dramatically, it's a good idea to keep the image selected and click the Resample button in the Pictures toolbar. Resampling adjusts the size of the pixels in the images so they match the new size. It can smooth out images that look jagged in appearance.

Positioning Images

The placement of images has a lot to do with how polished and professional a Web page looks. An image that wraps gracefully around adjacent text looks better than one that has simply been placed in the middle of the page with lots of empty space around it. Images should direct the eye toward accompanying headings or body text so people are encouraged to read about what they're seeing. FrontPage makes it easy to adjust image location to make a Web page communicate the message you want.

Position an Image

1 Select the image in your page, and click the Align Left, Center, or Align Right button. (Justify has no effect on images.)

2 Right-click the image in your page that you want to adjust and choose Picture Properties from the shortcut menu.

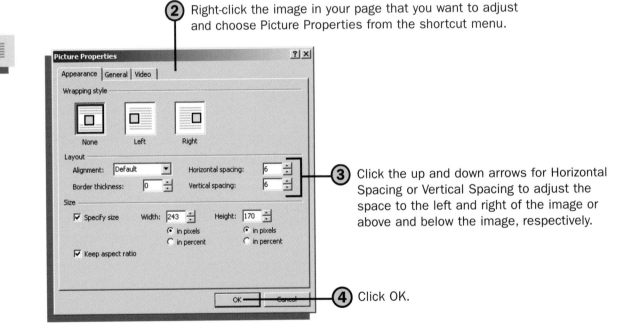

3 Click the up and down arrows for Horizontal Spacing or Vertical Spacing to adjust the space to the left and right of the image or above and below the image, respectively.

4 Click OK.

> **TIP:** If you want to make an image appear closer to surrounding text or other contents, enter a negative value in the Horizontal Spacing or Vertical Spacing box (such as −12, for example).

Wrap Text Around an Image

① Right-click the image in your page that you want to work with, and then select Picture Properties from the shortcut menu.

② Click the Appearance tab if it's not already selected.

! **TIP: Be sure to adjust horizontal spacing if you wrap text so there is some empty space between the image and surrounding text. Try adding six points of space, then adjust the spacing as needed.**

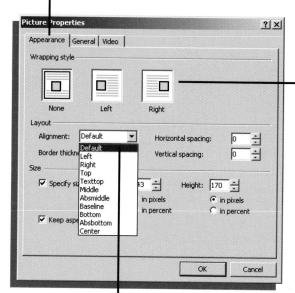

③ Click one of the three Wrapping Style options:

● To prevent text from wrapping around the image, select None.

● To place the image on the left and text on the right, select Left.

④ Click the Alignment drop-down list to position text more precisely.

● Right puts the image on the right and text on the left.

Adding Hotspots

Hyperlinks are one of the features that makes the Web unique and interactive, and parts of your Web page images can be made to take visitors to new locations with a single mouse click, too. A clickable region of an image that has been linked to a URL address is called a *hotspot*. It's possible to divide a single image into multiple hotspot areas. For example, you might publish an image of a house you're trying to sell, each window linked to a page containing photos of a specific room.

Create a Hotspot Link

① Select the image in your page.

② Click one of the Hotspot buttons on the Pictures toolbar—Rectangular, Circular, or Polygonal.

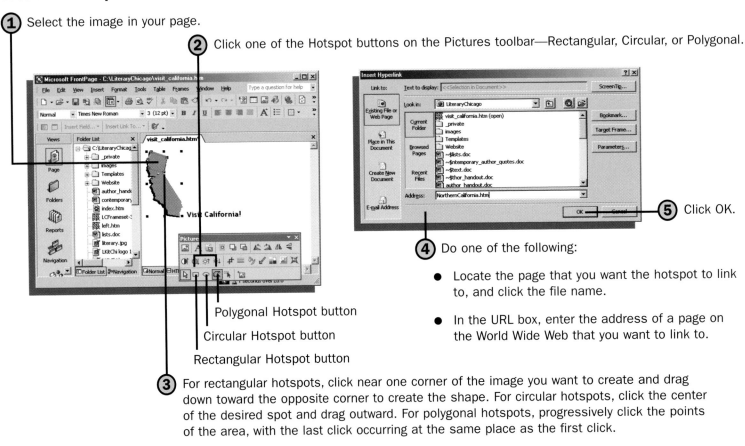

Polygonal Hotspot button

Circular Hotspot button

Rectangular Hotspot button

④ Do one of the following:

- Locate the page that you want the hotspot to link to, and click the file name.

- In the URL box, enter the address of a page on the World Wide Web that you want to link to.

⑤ Click OK.

③ For rectangular hotspots, click near one corner of the image you want to create and drag down toward the opposite corner to create the shape. For circular hotspots, click the center of the desired spot and drag outward. For polygonal hotspots, progressively click the points of the area, with the last click occurring at the same place as the first click.

Optimizing Images for the Web

You can never be sure exactly how people are going to view the Web pages you work so hard to create. They might be using different fonts than you intended; they might be using an old version of a browser that cannot display some advanced features; they might even be using a browser that doesn't display images at all. Creating textual alternates and low-resolution versions of your images will ensure that your message gets across even if viewers don't see the image you ideally want them to see.

Add Alternate Text

(1) Right-click an image in your page, and then select Picture Properties from the shortcut menu.

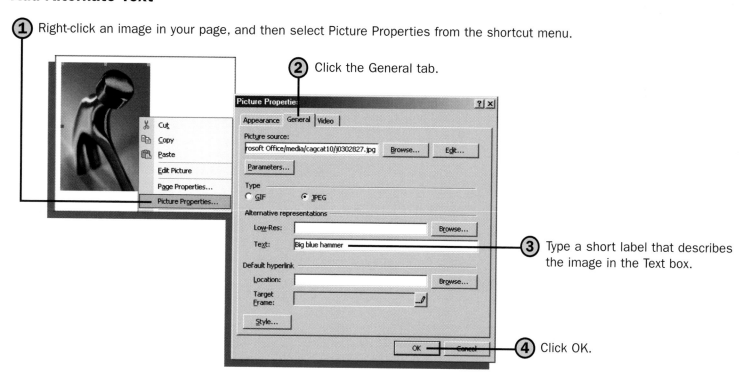

(2) Click the General tab.

(3) Type a short label that describes the image in the Text box.

(4) Click OK.

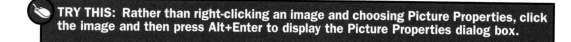

TRY THIS: Rather than right-clicking an image and choosing Picture Properties, click the image and then press Alt+Enter to display the Picture Properties dialog box.

Convert an Image to Grayscale

1 Select the image on your page that you want to convert.

2 Click the Color button, and then choose Grayscale from the shortcut menu.

! TIP: Text can be added to a picture by selecting the picture and then clicking the Text button on the Pictures toolbar. Though the words you type appear as text, they actually become part of the picture, so you have limited formatting capabilities.

SEE ALSO: If you want more control over the contrast or brightness of an image you convert to grayscale, use the contrast and brightness controls on the Pictures toolbar. See "Adjust a Thumbnail" on page 91 for more information.

! TIP: Wash Out, the other option that appears on the shortcut menu when you click Color, dramatically lightens the colors in an image. Washing out an image is useful when you want to type text on top of the image.

! TIP: If you don't like the grayscale or other effect you've applied, click the Restore button on the Pictures toolbar to restore the image to its original appearance.

Specify a Transparent Color

(1) Select a line art image on your page that has a solid background color.

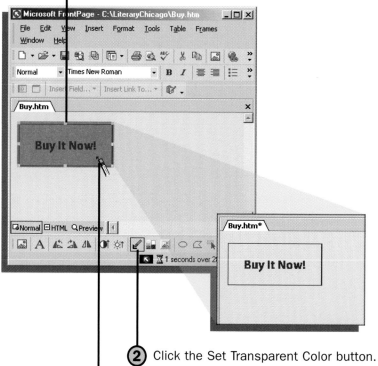

(2) Click the Set Transparent Color button.

(3) Move the pointer over the image—it now appears as a wand—and click the color in the image that you wish to make transparent.

TIP: If the image you're trying to make transparent is not in GIF format, you'll see a message prompting you to have FrontPage save the image as a GIF because the ability to make a color transparent is a feature of the GIF image compression format. **Click OK.**

CAUTION: If you add a line drawing from FrontPage's built-in clip art file, the image will already have transparency added. You don't need to select a transparent color for it. If you convert a clip art drawing from GIF to JPEG or another format, the image will lose its transparency.

Using Thumbnail Images

You are probably familiar with thumbnail images even if you're not sure what they are. If you've scanned through the clip art files in the Clip Organizer or the task pane, you've seen thumbnails—miniature representations of full-size images. By reducing a larger image to a postage stamp–sized thumbnail, you enable viewers to get a look at multiple images at once without consuming lots of memory.

Create a Thumbnail

(1) Select an image on your page.

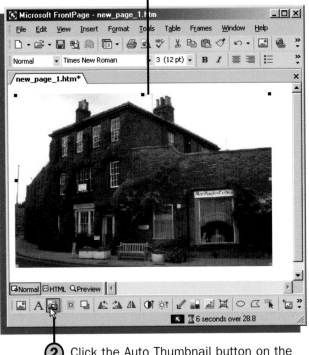

(2) Click the Auto Thumbnail button on the Pictures toolbar.

(3) Right-click the thumbnail, and then choose Follow Hyperlink from the shortcut menu to open the original image once again. (The thumbnail is automatically linked to the original.)

Adjust a Thumbnail

(1) Select the thumbnail.

TRY THIS: Need to create a clickable button? Either draw an image or select one from FrontPage's clip art files. Next create a thumbnail of the image with the Auto Thumbnail button. Then bevel the image with the Bevel button. You've got an instant button that you can link to a file to make it clickable.

(3) Click the More Brightness button as needed to increase the image's brightness.

(2) Click the More Contrast button repeatedly to increase contrast in the image.

TIP: Thumbnails you create with the Auto Thumbnail button automatically are displayed on the page with borders to signify that the image is actually a hyperlink—the thumbnail is linked to the full-size original.

Using Background Sound on a Web Page

Sound files can enliven and add a personal touch to any Web page. You've got two options for adding sound: You can make a link to an audio file so visitors can click the link and play the sound. (See "Adding Hyperlinks" on page 112.) You can also insert a background sound that automatically starts playing when a visitor's browser connects to a page. FrontPage has special controls for specifying the sound file to use and controlling how it is played.

Add a Background Sound

(1) Open the page that you want to include a background sound.

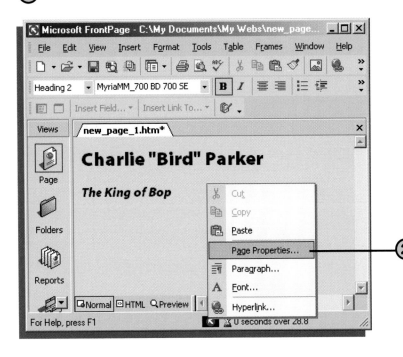

(2) Right-click the page, and choose Page Properties from the shortcut menu.

> **CAUTION:** Don't add a sound file just to entertain your visitors. They're just as likely to be annoyed by the unexpected music or other sounds coming from their computer. Background sounds should complement the contents of the page on which they appear. For instance, it makes sense to have a sample of their music playing in the background on a page about a musician or musical group.

③ Click the General tab.

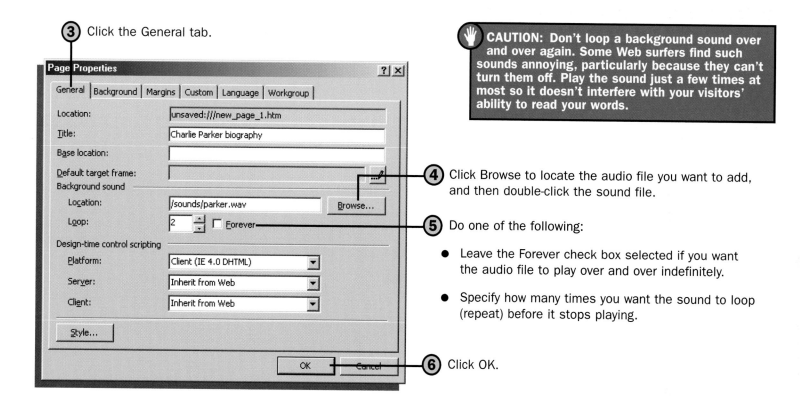

CAUTION: Don't loop a background sound over and over again. Some Web surfers find such sounds annoying, particularly because they can't turn them off. Play the sound just a few times at most so it doesn't interfere with your visitors' ability to read your words.

④ Click Browse to locate the audio file you want to add, and then double-click the sound file.

⑤ Do one of the following:

- Leave the Forever check box selected if you want the audio file to play over and over indefinitely.

- Specify how many times you want the sound to loop (repeat) before it stops playing.

⑥ Click OK.

TIP: Make sure the background sound you add isn't too large in size (say, no more than 50K in size). Otherwise users with slow modem connections will need several seconds to download the file, and they may have left the page before they even hear it.

Using Video on a Web Page

To make your Web page really come to life, you can add a video clip that will play when the viewer clicks a link. Usually, clicking a link tells the visitor's Web browser to launch a special application called a *plug-in,* which actually plays the image. Video clips take up large amounts of memory and work best for users who have fast Internet connections. You can help your users by setting properties for the video file and displaying controls to help them play the clip.

Add a Video Clip

(1) Open the Web page on which you want to include a video clip.

(2) Click to position the cursor where you want to include the video.

(3) Choose Video from the Picture submenu of the Insert menu.

(4) In the Look In drop-down list, locate the folder that contains the video clip you want to add.

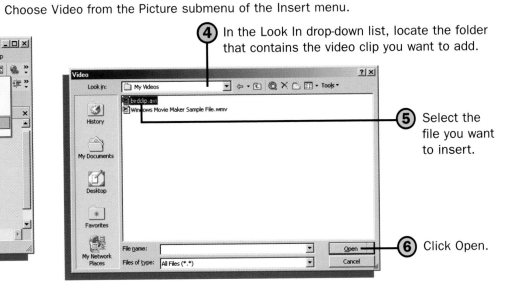

(5) Select the file you want to insert.

(6) Click Open.

! TIP: Once you set the properties for the video clip, test it out yourself to see how it looks. Click the Preview button to preview the page and play the video.

✔ SEE ALSO: Take into account the fact that some of your visitors won't be able to view the video file, due to either slow connections or browsers that don't support video. Include an alternate textual representation for the image, as explained in "Optimizing Images for the Web" on page 87.

Adjust Video File Properties

1 Right-click the video clip, and choose Picture Properties from the shortcut menu.

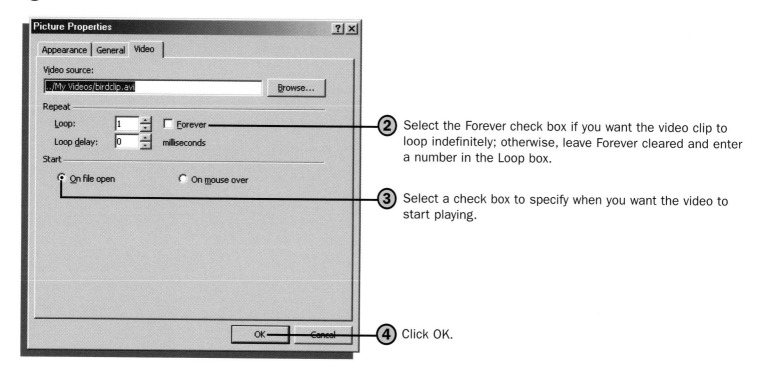

2 Select the Forever check box if you want the video clip to loop indefinitely; otherwise, leave Forever cleared and enter a number in the Loop box.

3 Select a check box to specify when you want the video to start playing.

4 Click OK.

6 Working with Tables

Tables aren't just for spreadsheets. With their orderly rows and columns, tables can help you organize contents on a Web page that don't fit neatly into lists or paragraphs of text. Tables can even add color to pages and enable you to come up with some complex design effects.

Tables can be used to line up rows of figures and columns of data. Rows and columns in a table are subdivided into individual containers called cells. Cells can contain text, numbers, images, background colors, and even other tables. Each cell has its own border, as does the table itself. You can control the size and the color of the border as well as the space between borders and text and between adjacent cells.

On the Web, tables are frequently used as layout devices. By adjusting the borders around the table cells, you can line up photos and text and divide pages into columns without making it obvious that a table is being used.

In this section, you learn how to create and edit tables, add borders and backgrounds, insert images, and change cell, row, and column size to fit your Web page design needs.

Creating a Table

If you tried to learn the HTML commands for creating and editing tables, you'd soon be awash in a sea of <TABLE>, <TR>, and <TD> codes. FrontPage takes care of arranging the rows and columns you need. One option is to create the table graphically, by clicking on the cells and rows you want your table to have. The other option is to actually draw the table outline in the FrontPage window. Either way, once you create the table, you'll find it easy to add content and edit the table to fit your needs.

Insert a Table

① Open the Web page on which you want the table to appear.

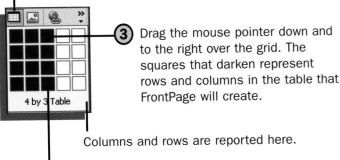

② Click the Insert Table button.

③ Drag the mouse pointer down and to the right over the grid. The squares that darken represent rows and columns in the table that FrontPage will create.

Columns and rows are reported here.

④ Release the mouse button to create the table.

> **TIP:** When you draw a table, the table's size is set as a fixed number of pixels. If the viewer makes his or her Web browser window smaller than either the height or the width of the table, some of it won't be visible. If you'd rather have the size of the table be relative to the page width, choose Table from the Insert submenu of the Table menu. For an existing table, right-click the table, select Table Properties from the shortcut menu, and then edit the Specify Width and Specify Height fields.

> **SEE ALSO:** You can choose from a set of preformatted table styles by clicking Table AutoFormat in the Tables toolbar and then selecting an option from the drop-down list. For more information, see "Automatically Formatting a Table" on page 109.

> **TIP:** You don't have to draw your table perfectly the first time. You can resize it whenever you want by clicking and dragging the right border to change the width or the bottom border to change the height. When you pass the mouse pointer over the right or the bottom border, it turns into a double-headed arrow. Dragging the bottom border resizes the bottom-most row. Use the Distribute Rows Evenly tool on the Tables toolbar to uniformly redistribute the row heights.

Draw a Table

1 Position the cursor at the spot where you want the table to appear.

2 Choose Draw Table from the Table menu. The Tables toolbar appears on your page.

3 Click and drag the mouse pointer (which turns into a pencil) down and to the right, and then release the mouse when the table's outer border is the size you want.

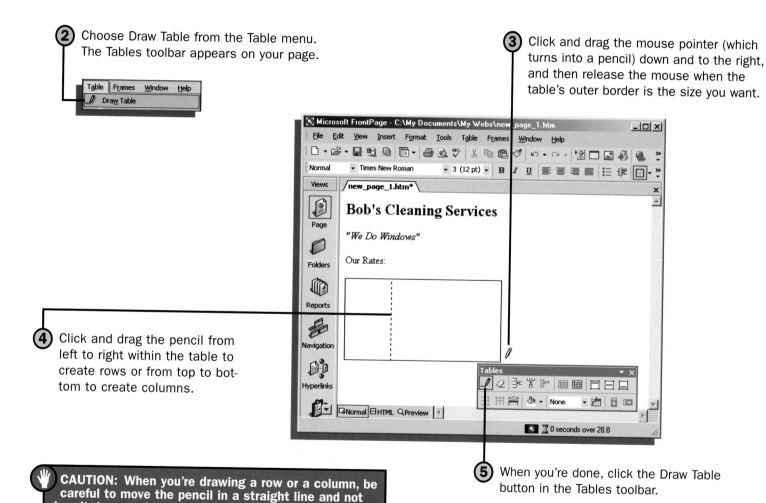

4 Click and drag the pencil from left to right within the table to create rows or from top to bottom to create columns.

5 When you're done, click the Draw Table button in the Tables toolbar.

CAUTION: When you're drawing a row or a column, be careful to move the pencil in a straight line and not drag it down and to the right, or FrontPage will think you're trying to draw a new table.

Insert a Row

TRY THIS: You can also add a single cell to a row or a column. Position the cursor in the cell to the right of where you want the new cell to appear. Then choose Cell from the Insert submenu of the Table menu.

1 Click to position the cursor in the row of the table below where you want the new row to appear.

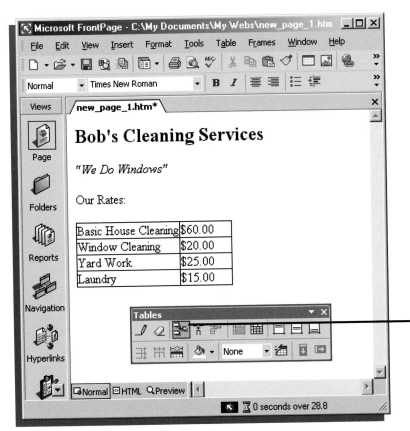

2 Do one of the following:

- Click the Insert Rows button in the Tables toolbar to add the new row above the current one.

- Choose Rows Or Columns from the Insert submenu of the Table menu, and then select the Rows option in the Insert Rows Or Columns dialog box.

Insert a Column

① Click to position the cursor in the column to the right of where you want the new column to appear.

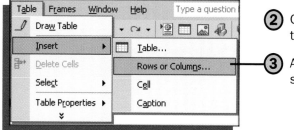

② Click the Insert Columns button in the Tables toolbar to add the new column to the left of the current one.

③ Alternatively, choose Rows Or Columns from the Insert submenu of the Table menu.

④ Select the Columns option.

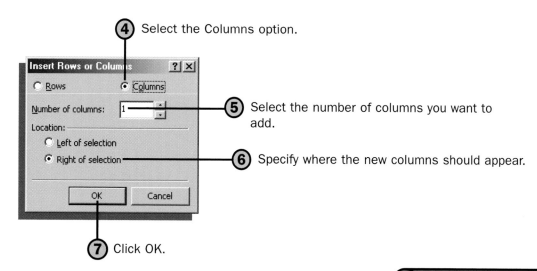

⑤ Select the number of columns you want to add.

⑥ Specify where the new columns should appear.

⑦ Click OK.

> **! TIP:** The Tables toolbar, which appears when you draw or insert a table, contains buttons that let you perform many of the same tasks covered in the Table menu. You can make the Tables toolbar visible any time you want by choosing Tables from the Toolbars submenu of the View menu.

> **✋ CAUTION:** If you use the Tables toolbar to add a row or a column, you can't control where the new row or column appears. The new row appears above the one where the cursor is positioned; the new column appears to the left of the current column. Choose Row Or Column from the Insert submenu of the Table menu if you want to have better control over where the new row or column appears.

Editing a Table

Information in tables doesn't need to be static. As the information changes, you can easily resize tables or rearrange them by deleting rows or columns. Unlike text or images, though, you can't usually delete parts of a table's structure simply by pressing the Delete key. Usually you need to select the part of the table you want to cut and then choose Delete Cells from the Table menu.

Delete a Row or Column

① Select the row or column by placing the cursor in a cell and then choosing Row Or Column from the Select submenu of the Table menu.

② Click the Delete Cells button in the Tables toolbar to delete the row or column.

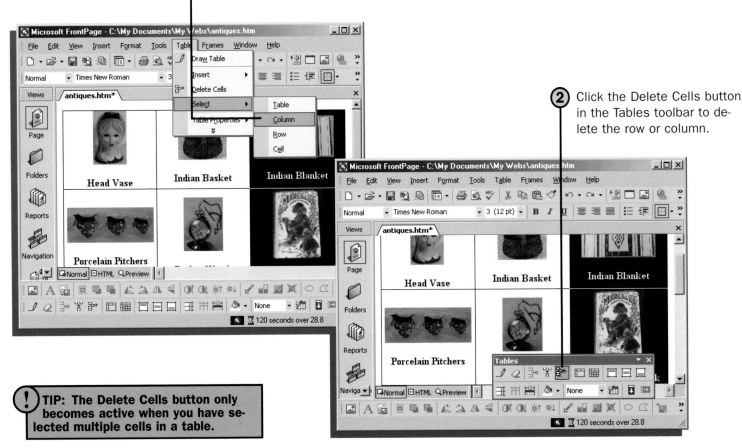

! TIP: The Delete Cells button only becomes active when you have selected multiple cells in a table.

Change Row Heights or Column Widths

(1) Pass your mouse pointer over the border between rows or columns until it becomes a double-headed arrow.

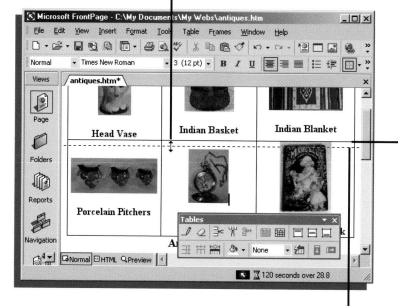

(2) Click on the border, and drag it to resize the row or column.

As you drag a border, it becomes a dashed line.

 SEE ALSO: For information on editing a table by adding or deleting rows or columns, see "Change the Layout" on page 107.

Split Cells

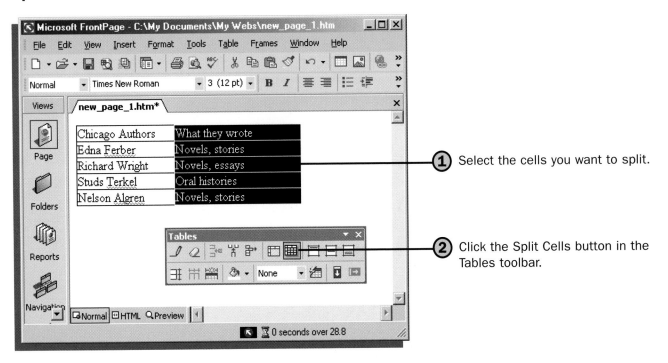

① Select the cells you want to split.

② Click the Split Cells button in the Tables toolbar.

③ Specify whether to split the cells into columns or rows.

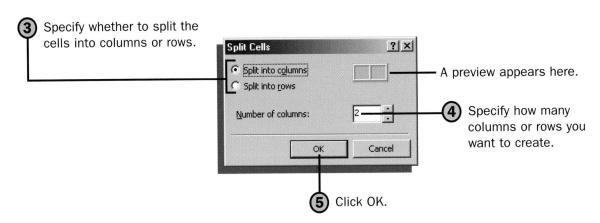

A preview appears here.

④ Specify how many columns or rows you want to create.

⑤ Click OK.

Combine Cells

(1) Select the cells you want to combine.

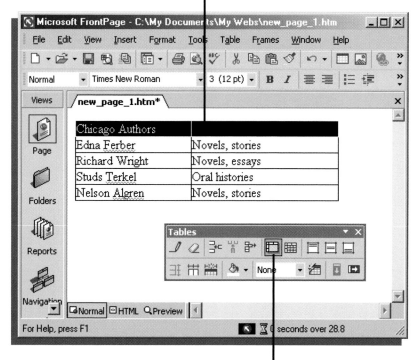

(2) Click the Merge Cells button in the Tables toolbar.

TRY THIS: You can merge cells by erasing the border between them. Click the Eraser button on the Tables toolbar, and then drag the pointer across the border once to erase it and merge the cells on either side.

Adding Text and Images to Cells

Once you have created a table and adjusted the structure to correspond to the information you want to present, you can add that information to the table's cells. You can add text, numbers, or images. The most obvious way to add text is to click in each cell and type the text. For images, you select the cell and use the Picture submenu of the Insert menu. You can also copy content from another program and paste it into the table.

Insert Text

(1) Select the cell where you want to add the text.

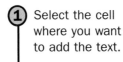

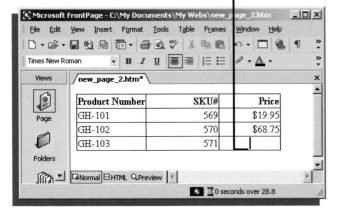

(2) Start typing.

! TIP: After you enter text in one cell, you can press Tab to move quickly to the next cell to the right.

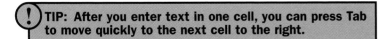

SEE ALSO: You can add any type of image to a cell, either from a file on your computer or on a network, from clip art, or from another Web page. For more information, see "Inserting Images" on page 72.

Insert an Image

(1) Select the cell.

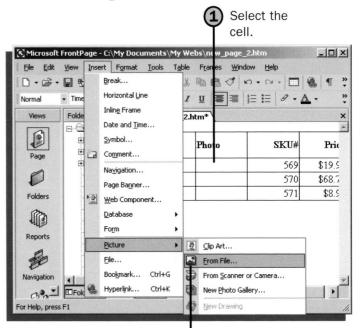

(2) Choose an option (Clip Art, From File, and so on) from the Picture submenu of the Insert menu.

! TIP: After you enter text in a cell, you can format the text using the controls in the Formatting toolbar or by choosing Font from the Format menu.

Changing a Cell's Appearance

Each cell within a table can have its own individual layout—its own height and width as well as border color and border thickness. By giving one or more cells a background color, you add graphic interest to your Web page. When you start to adjust the appearance of a table's cells, you really begin to fine-tune the way your information is presented.

Change the Layout

(1) Right-click the cell that you want to adjust.

(2) Choose Cell Properties from the shortcut menu.

(3) Choose an option from the Horizontal Alignment and Vertical Alignment drop-down lists to position the text or images in the cell.

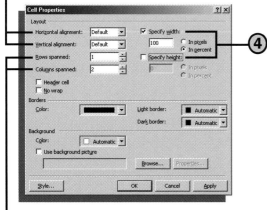

(4) Select the Specify Width and Specify Height check boxes, and enter values for the size of the cell.

(5) Click the Rows Spanned and Columns Spanned up and down arrows to change the number of columns or rows spanned by the cell.

(6) Click OK.

Add Cell Border Colors

(1) Right-click the cell, and choose Cell Properties from the shortcut menu.

(2) In the Borders area of the Cell Properties dialog box, select colors for the cell's borders. You have two choices:

- Choose an option from the Color drop-down list to make the cell's borders a single, solid color.

- Choose options from the Light Border and Dark Border drop-down list to give the cell border a shadow effect.

Changing a Table's Appearance

The process of adjusting the appearance of an entire table is similar to that for adjusting an individual cell. In this case, though, the tools can be found in the Table Properties dialog box rather than in the Cell Properties dialog box. By changing the size, color, and border style of your table, you make it fit in with the rest of the Web page's content and design.

Change the Layout

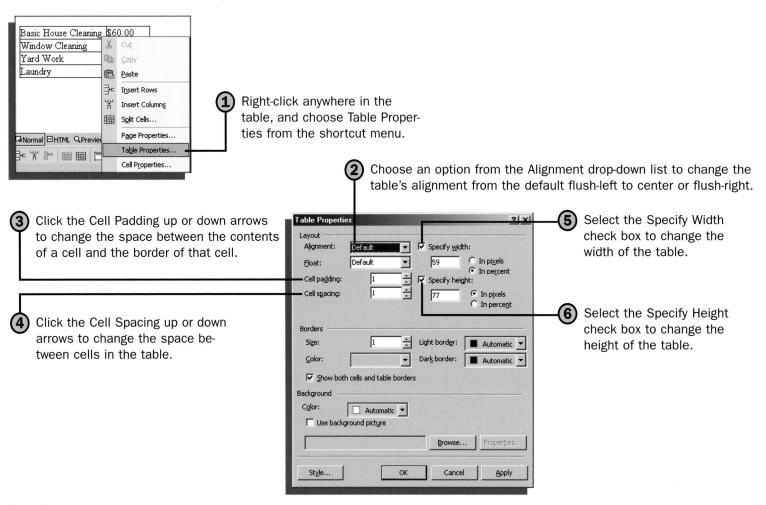

(1) Right-click anywhere in the table, and choose Table Properties from the shortcut menu.

(2) Choose an option from the Alignment drop-down list to change the table's alignment from the default flush-left to center or flush-right.

(3) Click the Cell Padding up or down arrows to change the space between the contents of a cell and the border of that cell.

(4) Click the Cell Spacing up or down arrows to change the space between cells in the table.

(5) Select the Specify Width check box to change the width of the table.

(6) Select the Specify Height check box to change the height of the table.

Automatically Formatting a Table

You don't have to do all the work of designing a table yourself. FrontPage has a number of options that can give you a jump start when you want to come up with an overall color, border style, and font combination for a table. You can also use some handy buttons in the Tables toolbar to fill out a table or automatically balance rows and columns.

Choose a Predesigned Table

(1) Click to position the cursor at the spot in the Web page where you want the table to appear.

(2) Click the Insert Table button, and drag to identify the cells you want your table to have.

(3) Click anywhere in the table you just created, and choose Table AutoFormat from the Table menu.

(4) Click a format in the Formats box.

(5) View a preview of the selected format in the Preview pane.

(6) Choose the table attributes you want the automatic table to include.

(7) Click OK.

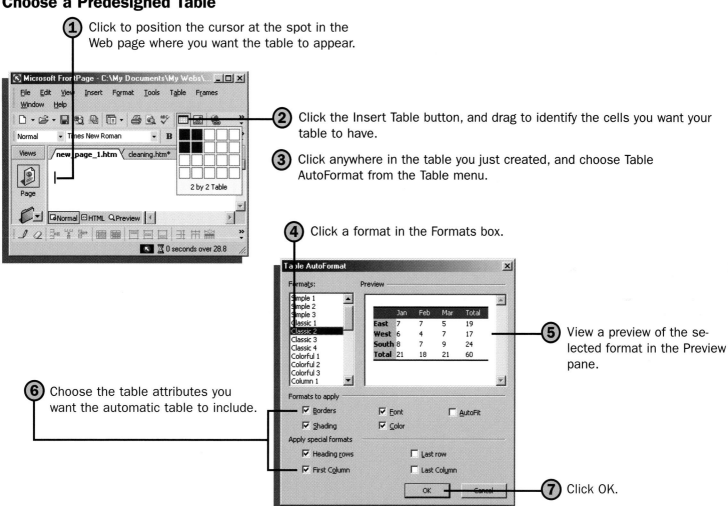

Using Navigation Elements

Hyperlinks provide the ability to locate files and objects by means of a standard address, and to jump from one location to another by clicking on links. Hyperlinks are the glue that links all the information in the World Wide Web together. And FrontPage is the tool that can help you add your own Web site to the incredible network of pages already linked to one another on the Web.

Creating hyperlinks to connect the individual files in your FrontPage-based Web is a snap. You begin by clicking the button called (intuitively enough) Insert Hyperlink. This opens a dialog box that helps you identify the destination of your link and gives you a place to add the address for that destination if you need to. You don't have to worry about the nuances of creating links in HTML.

Instead you can focus on making your links creative and easy for your visitors to use. You can use FrontPage to make the highlighted text links such as those you've probably clicked yourself as you've travelled around the Web. But you can also turn graphic images into links and create sets of clickable buttons called link bars.

In this section you explore the many tools FrontPage puts at your disposal for navigating your Web site. Of course, you get some experience working with hyperlinks, both to external files and to specific locations in the same document. You also discover some flashy navigation elements—shared borders, which give you sets of clickable buttons that appear the same from page to page; and Navigation View's site map, which gives you a visual representation of all the links in your site.

Adding Hyperlinks

Every link has two parts. The first is the starting point—the highlighted, clickable text or image that the viewer sees. The other part of a link, the destination, appears in the browser's status bar when the viewer passes the mouse pointer over the highlighted starting point. FrontPage enables you to join the two parts with user-friendly, graphical tools.

Link to an Existing File or Web Page

① Select the word or phrase that you want to be the clickable starting point for the link.

② Click the Insert Hyperlink button.

③ Click the Look In arrow to locate a file on your computer or network.

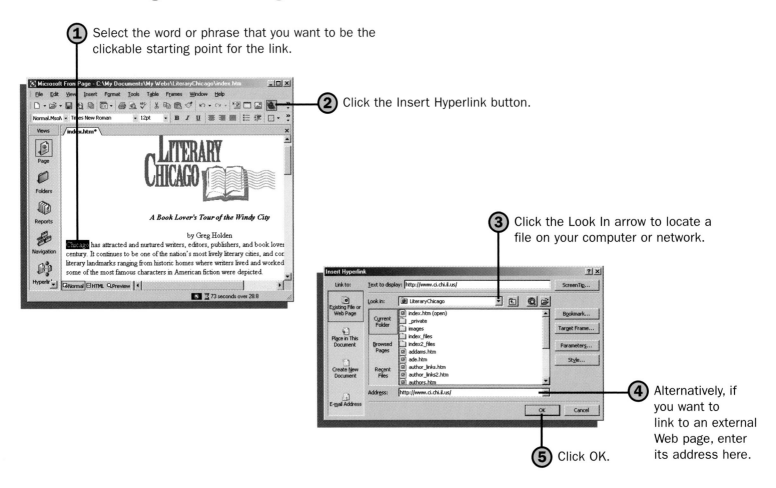

④ Alternatively, if you want to link to an external Web page, enter its address here.

⑤ Click OK.

Link to a Place in a Document

1. Create a bookmark by selecting an object for the link's destination.

2. Choose Bookmark from the Insert menu.

SEE ALSO: The process of creating textual links is almost identical to adding hot spots to an image. In either case, you use the Insert Hyperlink dialog box to link to existing files, bookmarks, or e-mail addresses. See "Adding and Editing Hot Spots" on page 86 for more information.

TIP: In case you have the Standard toolbar hidden and the Insert Hyperlink button isn't visible, you can also access the Insert Hyperlink dialog box by right-clicking the text you've highlighted and choosing Hyperlink from the shortcut menu.

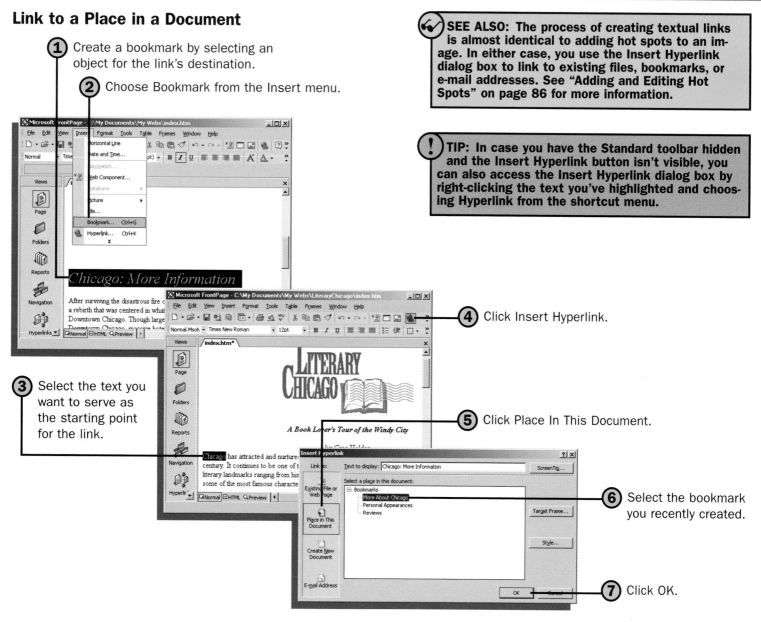

4. Click Insert Hyperlink.

3. Select the text you want to serve as the starting point for the link.

5. Click Place In This Document.

6. Select the bookmark you recently created.

7. Click OK.

Link to an E-Mail Address

1 Right-click the highlighted text, and then choose Hyperlink from the shortcut menu.

2 Click E-Mail Address.

3 Enter the e-mail address to which you want users to send e-mail.

4 Alternatively, select a recently used e-mail address if you want to use one.

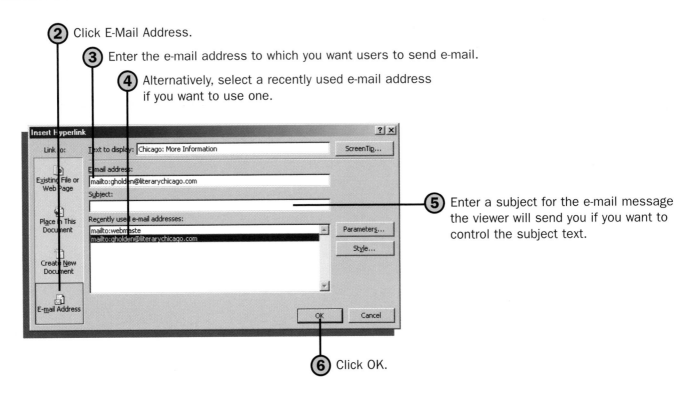

5 Enter a subject for the e-mail message the viewer will send you if you want to control the subject text.

6 Click OK.

Turning an Image into a Hyperlink

FrontPage makes it easy to turn an image into a clickable link. You can link an image to a Web page, an e-mail address, or a bookmark. Clicking the image takes the viewer to the new location. Clickable images are important both from a navigational and business standpoint—they are frequently used to create link bars (rows of clickable buttons) as well as banner ads that take viewers from one Web site to an advertiser's site with a single mouse click.

Create a Clickable Image Link

① Select the image.

② Click the Insert Hyperlink button.

③ Click one of the buttons in the Link To column to select the type of link you want to create.

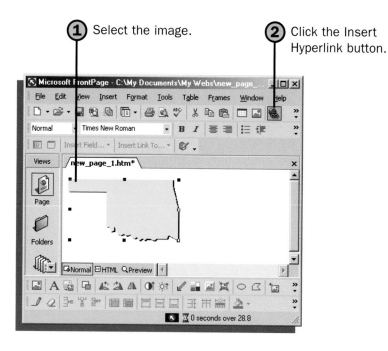

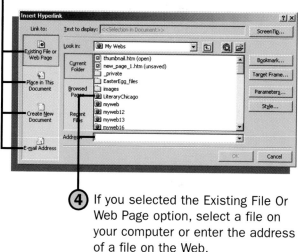

④ If you selected the Existing File Or Web Page option, select a file on your computer or enter the address of a file on the Web.

⑤ Click OK.

> **TRY THIS:** By default, an image that has been linked to another file does not contain a visible border. The only way a viewer knows that the image is a link is because the URL appears in a browser's status bar when the mouse pointer passes over the image. To add a border to the image to make it more obvious that the image is clickable, select the image, choose Borders And Shading from the Format menu, click Box, and click OK. (You might have to click on the border to resize it to fit correctly around the image.)

Editing Hyperlinks

Part of your ongoing Web site maintenance—and it's a good idea to update and check your site regularly after it goes on line—should be to edit your hyperlinks. FrontPage makes editing links as easy as it was to create them in the first place.

Change a Link

(1) Right-click the link.

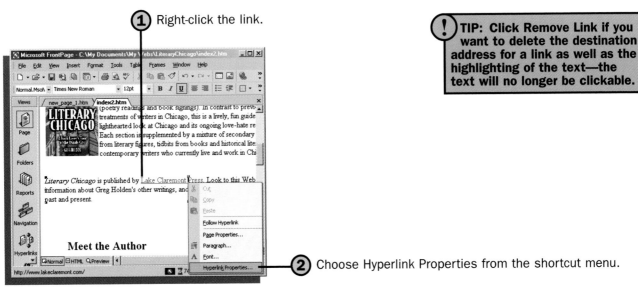

> ! **TIP: Click Remove Link if you want to delete the destination address for a link as well as the highlighting of the text—the text will no longer be clickable.**

(2) Choose Hyperlink Properties from the shortcut menu.

(3) Enter a new address.

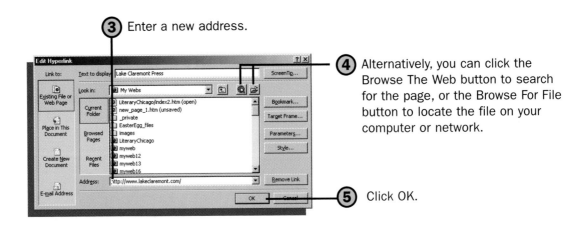

(4) Alternatively, you can click the Browse The Web button to search for the page, or the Browse For File button to locate the file on your computer or network.

(5) Click OK.

Change Hyperlink Colors

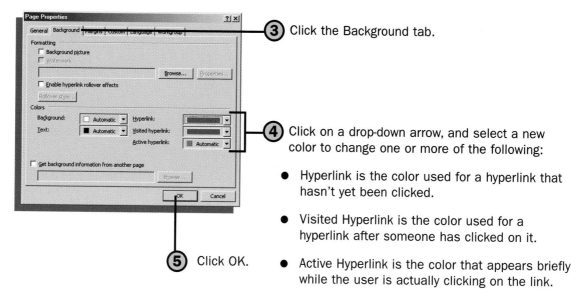

① Right-click anywhere in the Web page.

② Choose Page Properties from the shortcut menu.

③ Click the Background tab.

④ Click on a drop-down arrow, and select a new color to change one or more of the following:

● Hyperlink is the color used for a hyperlink that hasn't yet been clicked.

● Visited Hyperlink is the color used for a hyperlink after someone has clicked on it.

⑤ Click OK.

● Active Hyperlink is the color that appears briefly while the user is actually clicking on the link.

Using Bookmarks

Like a slip of paper you place in between the pages of a printed book, a bookmark on a Web page is a marker you create with FrontPage so that you can return to that spot by making a link to it. A link to a bookmark helps your visitors navigate your FrontPage-based Web by enabling them to jump to the location they need to find out a bit of information. A bookmark enables visitors to link to text in the same page as the link they clicked on.

Add a Bookmark

(1) Open the Web page on which you want to create a bookmark.

(2) Position the cursor at the spot in the page where you want to create the bookmark.

(3) Choose Bookmark from the Insert menu.

(4) Type a short, descriptive name for the bookmark in the Bookmark Name text box.

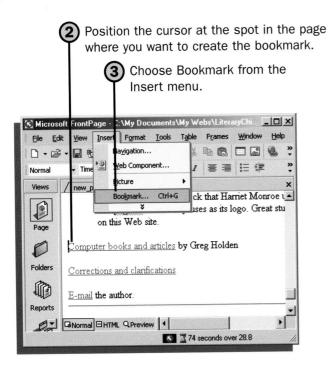

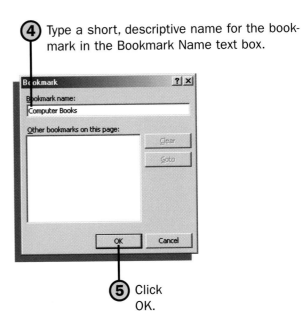

(5) Click OK.

Delete a Bookmark

(1) Right-click the bookmark.

Literary Chicago combines anecdotes and excerpts d
with walking tours that guide readers to historic sites, s
present literary hangouts, and current events for reader

Gregory Holden is a life-long resident of the Chica
Degree in English and Writing from the University of Ill
Holden has been a full-time writer of books on comput
on the city's North Side.

(2) Choose Bookmark Properties
from the shortcut menu.

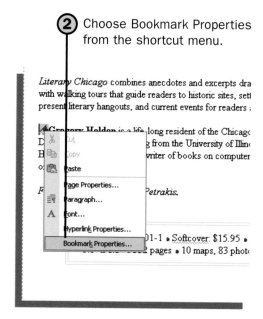

(3) Select the bookmark from the Other
Bookmarks On This Page list box.

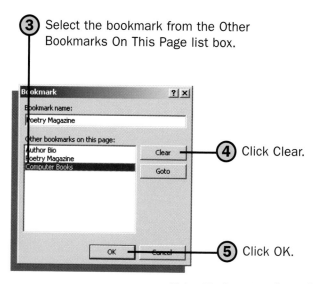

(4) Click Clear.

(5) Click OK.

Working with Shared Borders

Good Web sites are marked not only by having a single owner and a shared home page, but also by consistent design and navigation elements. Shared borders give you the chance to create a graphically interesting navigation tool that you can use either on a single Web page or on all the pages in your site. All of the site's pages can "share" a title bar, a set of navigation buttons, and contact information.

Create a Shared Border

1 Open the Web site in which you want to create shared borders.

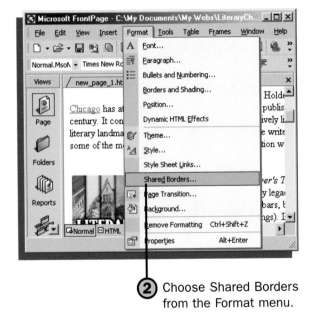

2 Choose Shared Borders from the Format menu.

3 Click All Pages to apply the borders to all pages on the site.

4 Alternatively, click Current Page to apply the borders only to the current page.

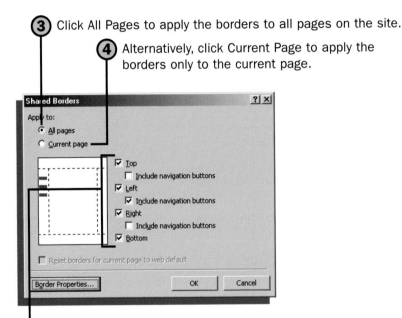

5 Click one or more of the following border options:

● Top places a border at the top of the Web page and is often used for the site's banner.

● Bottom places a border at the bottom of the page, the logical location for contact and copyright information.

● Left and Right place borders at the respective vertical margins.

● Include Navigation Buttons creates a set of clickable buttons in the top, left-hand, or right-hand border.

Change Shared Border Text

1 Single-click the existing text to select it all at once.

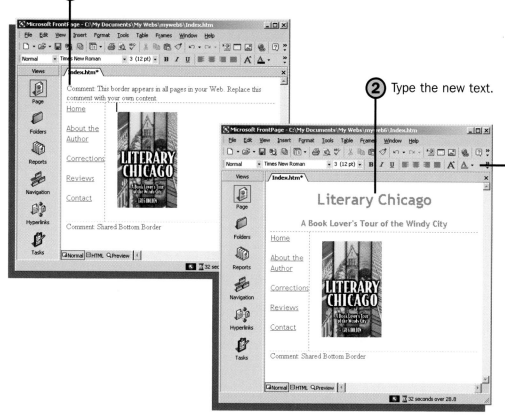

2 Type the new text.

3 Select heading styles and other formatting attributes from the Formatting toolbar.

✋ **CAUTION:** Although you can add navigation buttons to the top, left, and right shared borders at the same time, it only makes sense to put the buttons in one of these locations. The convention used on many Web pages is to place the buttons in the left-hand shared border.

⚠ **TIP:** Shared borders have some advantages over frames—subdivisions of a Web page that can be set up to create a set of navigational links and a page title that stay in one place while the viewer clicks on links to switch from page to page. Frames pages can take several seconds or more to load in their entirety, and some older or non-graphical browsers don't support them. In contrast, shared borders work with all browsers.

Viewing Hyperlinks

It can be difficult to keep track of all the hyperlinks in a Web site, particularly when the site gets very large and complex. For corporate sites, it's sometimes helpful to be able to display or print out a visual representation of how the pages in a site are linked to one another. The FrontPage Hyperlinks view gives you a visual representation of how any one page in your site is linked to its companion pages.

Review Hyperlinks

① Open the page that you want to check.

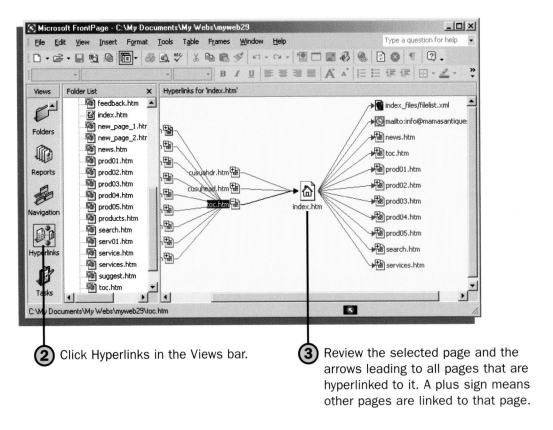

② Click Hyperlinks in the Views bar.

③ Review the selected page and the arrows leading to all pages that are hyperlinked to it. A plus sign means other pages are linked to that page.

Test Hyperlinks

① Open the page with the link you want to check.

② Click Page to go to Page view.

③ Press Ctrl, and click on a link to follow it.

④ When the linked page or file opens in the FrontPage window, verify that it's the correct destination.

! TIP: Right-click one of the hyperlink arrows in Navigation view and a shortcut menu appears with options for editing the hyperlinks that are displayed. Choose Show Page Titles to view the titles of the hyperlinked pages, Hyperlinks To Pictures to display links to images as well as pages, or Repeated Hyperlinks to show all instances of hyperlinks that are made more than once.

SEE ALSO: FrontPage gives you the ability to verify all of the hyperlinks in a Web site at once. For more information, see "Verifying Hyperlinks" on page 206.

Working with Navigation View

In order to make it easy for visitors to get around your Web site, you've first got to get a clear view of your site's structure yourself. With Navigation view, FrontPage gives you a way to view the organization of your site as a "tree," with top-level pages, the second-level pages linked to them, the third-level pages linked to them, and so on.

Review the Web Site Structure

1 Open the site you want to view.

2 Click Navigation in the Views bar.

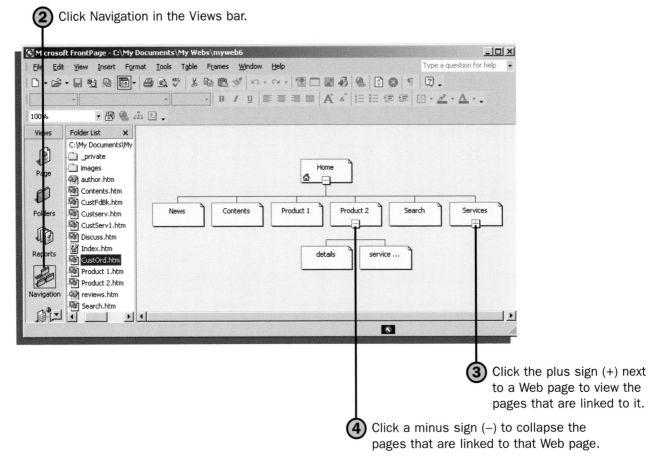

3 Click the plus sign (+) next to a Web page to view the pages that are linked to it.

4 Click a minus sign (–) to collapse the pages that are linked to that Web page.

Customize Navigation View

(1) If you can't see all your site's pages on one screen, choose Size To Fit from the drop-down list in the Navigation toolbar.

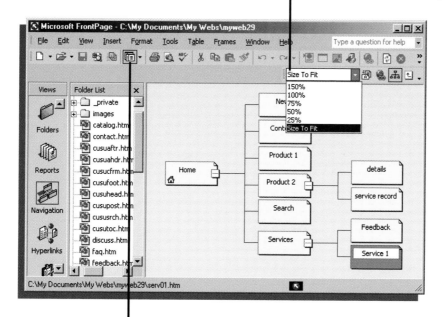

(2) Click here to toggle the display of the Folder List.

⊘ TRY THIS: If your screen space is limited, you can hide the Navigation toolbar by choosing Navigation from the Toolbars submenu of the View menu. Then right-click anywhere in the blank area of Navigation view (not on a page icon) and choose an option from the shortcut menu. (All of the Navigation toolbar options except Add Existing Page are included in this shortcut menu plus an additional option, Expand All, which shows all linked pages in the Web. The Add Existing Page option is available in the shortcut menu displayed by right-clicking a page icon in Navigation view.)

⚠ TIP: The drop-down menu lets you choose other zoom options for Navigation view; you can blow the view up by 150% or reduce it to as little as 25% of the original size.

Add a Page in Navigation View

(1) Open the Web site in Navigation view.

(2) Click one of the page icons to select it. (This activates the remaining Navigation toolbar buttons.)

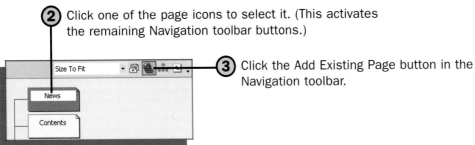

(3) Click the Add Existing Page button in the Navigation toolbar.

(4) Locate the folder that contains the file you want to add.

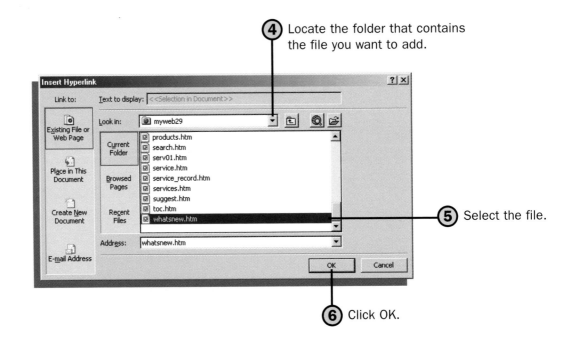

(5) Select the file.

(6) Click OK.

Using Frames

F rames enable you to take the organization and interactivity of your FrontPage-based Web to a new level. A Web page that's been divided into frames is like a television screen that's been split so you can watch what's happening in two or more locations at once: each Web page frame is a Web page in its own right. Each frame, then, can contain its own combination of text, images, and hyperlinks.

One frame can contain the banner image, including the name of a Web site; another can contain a set of hyperlinks; another can contain the copyright and contact information for the site; and another, larger frame can serve as the main viewing area where visitors read the text and images.

To this point, frames probably sound a bit like shared borders. But frames can do some things that no other Web page layout approach can touch. For one thing, frames can interact with one another—a link in one frame can be targeted so that the file associated with the link appears in another frame. Frames can have borders that the viewer can resize; you can also set up frames so the borders don't resize or there are no visible borders at all.

In this section, you learn how to create a frames layout using one of the FrontPage templates. You discover how to edit a frame's content as well as its properties. For instance, you'll see how to split a frame, how to control whether scroll bars appear, how to give a visitor an alternative to viewing frames, and how to use frames without visible borders.

Creating Frames

FrontPage gives you a jump-start in creating frames pages by providing a variety of templates from which to choose. By setting up a frames structure for you, FrontPage lets you focus on the content you want to create. Before you choose a template, it's a good idea to sketch out your frames first on paper. Determine what kind of content each frame should contain. When you browse through the templates, you'll be more likely to pick one that's just right for your site.

Choose a Frame Page Template

(1) Choose Page Or Web from the New submenu of the File menu.

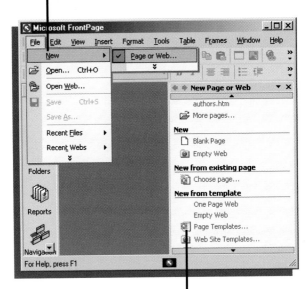

(2) Click Page Templates in the New From Template section of the Task Pane.

(3) Click the Frames Pages tab.

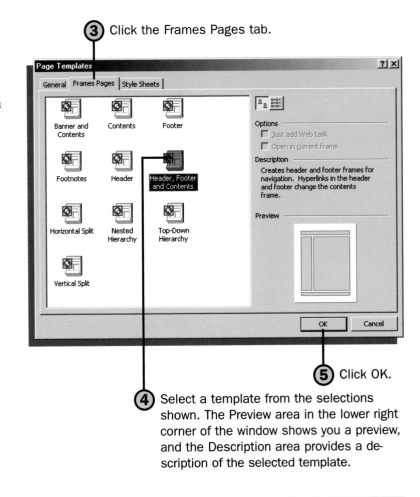

(5) Click OK.

(4) Select a template from the selections shown. The Preview area in the lower right corner of the window shows you a preview, and the Description area provides a description of the selected template.

> ✋ **CAUTION:** Shared borders divide a page into separate areas, much like frames. Avoid using a frames layout in a site that already has shared borders applied to it—you'll confuse your viewers. A link bar performs the same task as a frame that contains a set of links. Avoid using a link bar on a frame page, also.

Anatomy of a Frames Page

A frames page contains a different set of elements than a single non-frames Web page, but the elements are ones you should be familiar with. There are many different kinds of possible frames layouts, but they contain the standard elements seen in this figure.

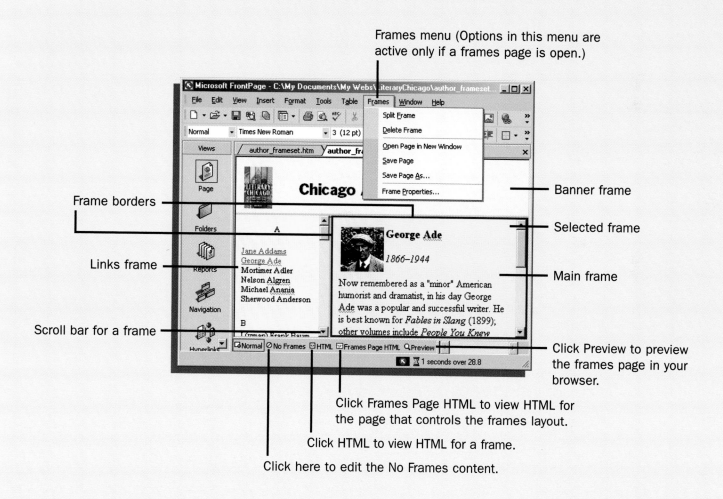

Frames menu (Options in this menu are active only if a frames page is open.)

Frame borders

Links frame

Scroll bar for a frame

Banner frame

Selected frame

Main frame

Click Preview to preview the frames page in your browser.

Click Frames Page HTML to view HTML for the page that controls the frames layout.

Click HTML to view HTML for a frame.

Click here to edit the No Frames content.

Adding Content to Frames

Once you've selected a frames template and created a page that's been divided into frames, the next step is to add content to those frames. You've got to edit each page individually; remember, each frame is a Web page in its own right. You can assign a new page to a frame and edit it from scratch; you can also identify an existing page and insert that in the frame.

Insert an Existing Page in a Frame

1 Open the frames page you want to edit.

2 Click a frame to select it. A selected frame has a dark blue border around it.

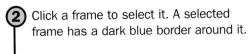

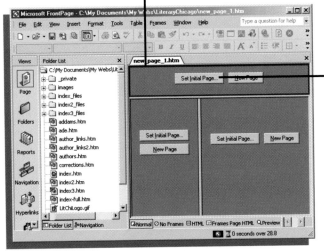

3 Click Set Initial Page.

SEE ALSO: When you identify an existing file and add it to a frame, it becomes the first page to appear in that frame. But it's not necessarily the last. If you make a hyperlink in one frame and target another frame, the content of the frame changes to display a new Web page. See "Targeting a Frame" on page 138 for more information.

4 In the Insert Hyperlink dialog box, select a file and click OK to insert the file into the selected frame.

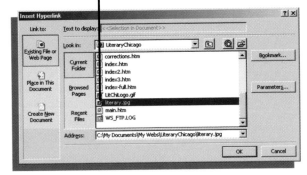

CAUTION: Some browsers don't support frames. For those users with older versions of browsers or with non-graphical browsers, you need to create an alternate version of the frames layout, or at the very least, ensure the No Frames message, accessed from the No Frames tab in Page view, states that "your browser does not support frames." It's a little extra work, but it's better than having users see nothing at all when they attempt to view your frames page.

Resize a Frame

(1) If the page you add doesn't exactly match the frame's size, click on the frame border and drag it to enlarge or reduce the frame size.

(!) TIP: If you click the Show All button in the Standard toolbar, FrontPage displays paragraph markers, line breaks, and other symbols not only in the currently selected frame but also in all of the page's frames.

Add a New Page to a Frame

(1) Open the frames page you want to edit.

(4) When the blank page appears within the frame, begin typing.

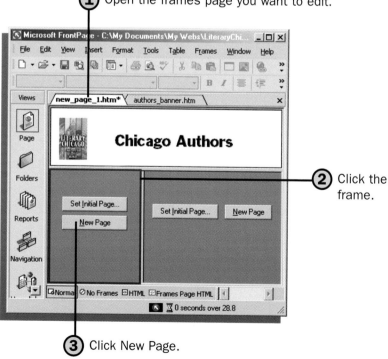

(2) Click the frame.

(3) Click New Page.

(5) Format the frame like any other Web page—format text, press Return to create new paragraphs, and add hyperlinks as needed.

Saving Frames Pages

Saving pages in a frames layout involves a few more steps than simply saving a normal Web page. You have to save each page in the layout individually—not the frames themselves, but the pages contained within the frames. (The frames themselves are simply containers and not separate files.) You also have to save the frames page, which is the page that includes the formatting instructions for the entire frameset.

Save a Page in a Frame

① Having selected the frame that contains the file you want to save, choose Save Page As from the Frames menu.

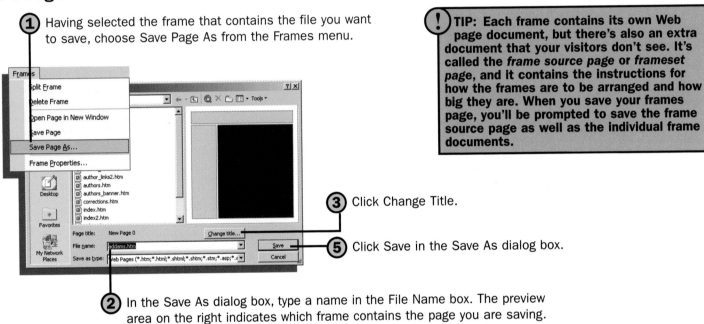

TIP: Each frame contains its own Web page document, but there's also an extra document that your visitors don't see. It's called the *frame source page* or *frameset page*, and it contains the instructions for how the frames are to be arranged and how big they are. When you save your frames page, you'll be prompted to save the frame source page as well as the individual frame documents.

③ Click Change Title.

⑤ Click Save in the Save As dialog box.

② In the Save As dialog box, type a name in the File Name box. The preview area on the right indicates which frame contains the page you are saving.

④ Type a title for the page in the Set Page Title dialog box, and then click OK.

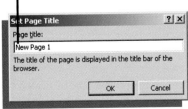

TIP: Choose Save All from the File menu if you'd like to save all of the pages in a frameset at once. Otherwise, you have to select each frame individually and choose Save (if you've saved the page before) or Save As (if you are saving the page for the first time).

Save the Frames Page

(1) With the frames page open, choose Save As from the File menu.

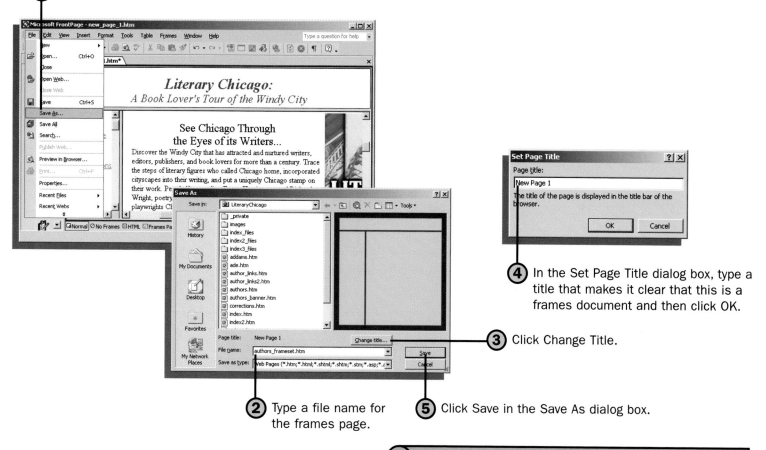

(4) In the Set Page Title dialog box, type a title that makes it clear that this is a frames document and then click OK.

(3) Click Change Title.

(2) Type a file name for the frames page.

(5) Click Save in the Save As dialog box.

CAUTION: By default, a frames page is given the generic file name "new_page_1.htm." If you choose Save from the File menu, you'll save the frames page with this name. To give the frames page a more descriptive name so that you can find it more easily later on, choose Save As from the File menu.

TIP: The file name of a page is different from the title. The file name is the name that appears in the Folder List or in Windows Explorer. The title is the text that appears in the top bar of the viewer's browser window. Titles are important because they're used by Internet search engines to index your pages. Take the time to choose a short, descriptive title that describes each page's contents.

Adjusting a Frameset's Properties

If you know some HTML, you can view the HTML for the frameset and edit the source code directly, but FrontPage makes it easy to change a frame's or frameset's properties without even looking at the HTML. A set of frames (or *frameset*) has a frames page that controls their overall arrangement, so you can often customize the frames by editing the frames page.

Adjust Frame Margins

1 Right-click the frame, and then choose Frame Properties from the shortcut menu.

2 In the Margins section of the Frame Properties dialog box, use the Width box to specify a size (in pixels) for the margin to the left and right of the frame's contents.

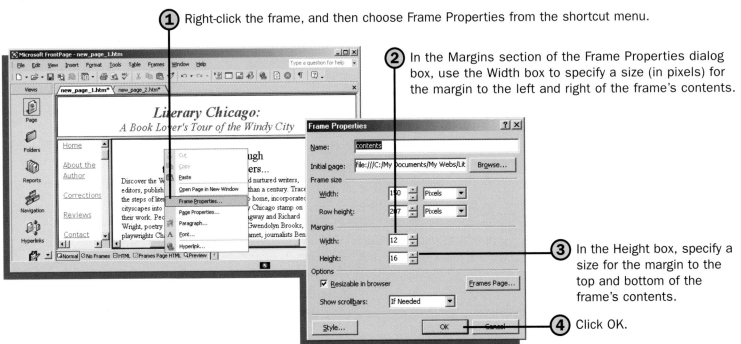

3 In the Height box, specify a size for the margin to the top and bottom of the frame's contents.

4 Click OK.

TRY THIS: Each page in a frame can have a different background color if you want. Right-click the frame, and then choose Page Properties from the shortcut menu. When the Page Properties dialog box appears, click Background and then select a color from the drop-down list next to Background.

SEE ALSO: You can always add hyperlinks to a page in a frame—see "Adding Hyperlinks" on page 112 for more information. You can add images, too, but if the frame you're using is small in height or width, make sure any image you add is going to appear in its entirety. If not, drag the frame's border to resize it. See "Inserting Images" on page 71 for more on working with images.

Change the Space Between Frames

(1) Open the frameset you want to edit.

(2) Choose Frame Properties from the Frames menu.

(3) Click the Frames Page button.

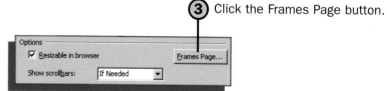

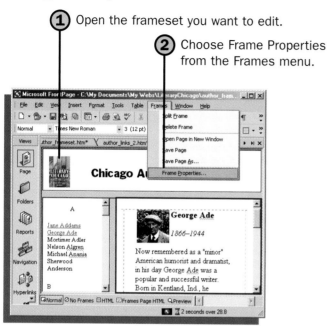

(4) Specify a size (in pixels) for the space between frames—which is also the width of the borders between frames.

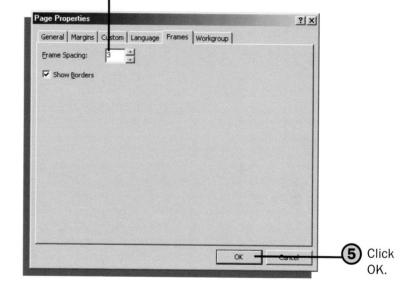

(5) Click OK.

TRY THIS: If you're feeling adventurous or just want to get a glimpse of how frames are arranged in HTML, open a frames page and click the Frames Page HTML button to view the source code. The instructions for the arrangement of frames in the frameset are contained in the command *<frameset> </frameset>*. The *rows=x,x* command tells you how many rows are in the frameset and how big they are. The *cols=x,x* command tells you how many columns there are in the frameset and how big they are. By changing the number x in *framespacing="x"*, you can change the space between frames.

SEE ALSO: Give your viewers more than just the default "noframes" message to view. You can provide an alternate arrangement for the entire frameset by replacing the default message with new content. You could use tables to provide another version of the frames page, for instance. See "Creating a Table" on page 98 for more information.

Adjusting a Frame's Properties

The Frame Properties dialog box contains a wealth of options for controlling exactly how an individual frame appears. You not only have control over the frame's size and the file it contains, but also over whether the frame should be resizeable by the viewer or "frozen" in the size you want.

Change a Frame's Properties

(1) Right-click the frame you want to edit, and then choose Frame Properties from the shortcut menu.

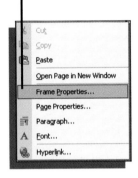

(2) You can change the name of the selected frame by typing a new name in the Name text box.

(3) Click Browse, and locate a new file to display in the frame, if you want to.

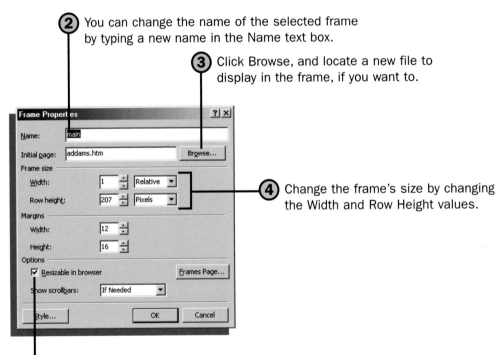

(4) Change the frame's size by changing the Width and Row Height values.

(5) Uncheck Resizable In Browser if you want the frame's dimensions to be fixed. If the entire frames page is selected, this setting affects all the frames on the page, making them impossible for the viewer to resize.

Show or Hide Frame Borders

1 In the Frame Properties dialog box for a selected frame, click Frames Page.

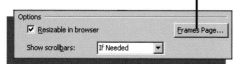

2 Uncheck the Show Borders check box.

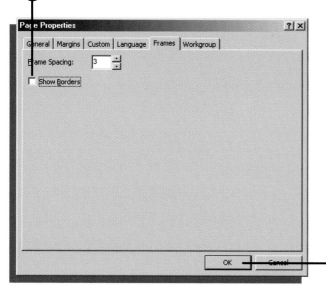

4 To view the new borderless frames page, click Preview to display the frames page in your browser.

3 Click OK to close Page Properties, and then click OK to close Frame Properties.

① TIP: Even if you make borders invisible on a frame, you can still see them when you work on the page in the FrontPage Normal view window. The "invisible" frame border appears as a thin gray line that you can drag if you need to resize the frame.

✋ CAUTION: Frames without visible borders can be confusing for your visitors—particularly if some of the adjacent frames still have visible scroll bars. Unless you have a compelling reason to delete borders, you should avoid doing so.

Targeting a Frame

Frames pages really show their worth when you make them interact with one another. FrontPage makes it easy to target a frame so that a link in one frame causes the linked content to appear in another frame. You only need to know two things: the name of the frame you want to target, and the name of the file you want to link to that frame.

Rename a Frame

① Right-click the frame you want to target, and then choose Frame Properties from the shortcut menu.

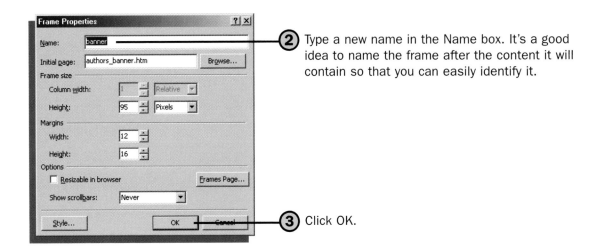

② Type a new name in the Name box. It's a good idea to name the frame after the content it will contain so that you can easily identify it.

③ Click OK.

TIP: When a frames page is first opened, the entire frames page is selected. If you've selected a specific frame, you can reselect the entire frames page by holding down the Shift key while clicking on any frame border.

TIP: Among the frame target options, New Window means the linked file will appear in a new window instead of a frame. Same Frame means the linked content will appear in the same frame as the link.

Identify a Target Frame

① Right-click the link you want to target.

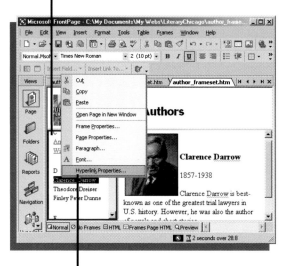

② Choose Hyperlink Properties from the shortcut menu.

③ In the Edit Hyperlink dialog box, make sure the file listed in the Address box is the one you want to appear in the targeted frame.

④ Click Target Frame.

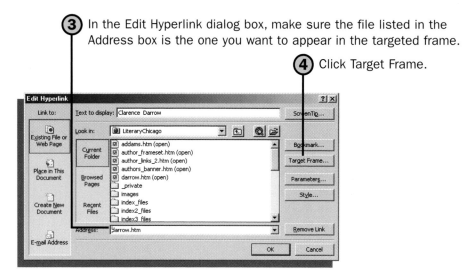

⑤ In the Target Frame dialog box, click the frame where you want the linked file to appear or select one of the options listed to the right.

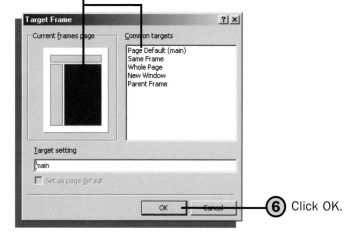

⑥ Click OK.

Splitting and Deleting Frames

Your first choice for a frames layout doesn't need to be the permanent one. You can easily rearrange your frames by splitting them (turning one frame into two) or deleting them. Simply deleting the content in a frame doesn't delete the frame itself; if you want to delete the frame, you need to use the Frames menu.

Split a Frame

1 Click a frame to select it.

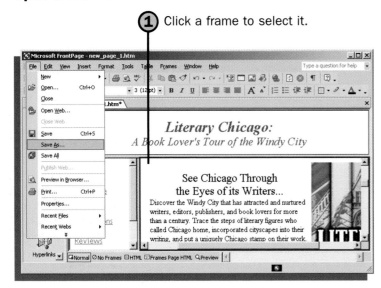

2 Choose Split Frame from the Frames menu.

3 Specify whether you want to split the frame vertically or horizontally, and then click OK. The frame splits into two equal halves.

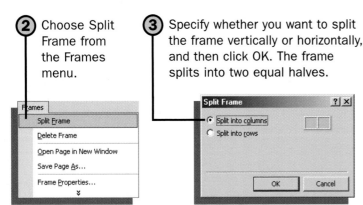

Delete a Frame

1 Select the frame.

2 Choose Delete Frame from the Frames menu.

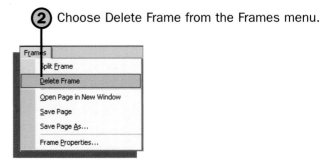

CAUTION: You can split frames as often as you wish, but remember that when someone wants to view your frames page, the browser has to load each page separately. If your page contains five, six, or even more frames, the page can take a long time to appear, which can be frustrating for Web surfers with slow connections.

TIP: If you've deleted other frames and only one remains, you cannot delete that frame by choosing Delete Frame from the Frames menu. If you really want to delete the page, right-click the page in the Folder List and choose Delete from the shortcut menu.

TRY THIS: For another method of splitting a frame, press the CTRL key and drag the frame's border. This option allows you to control the size of the new frame.

Using Web Components and Effects

 NEW FEATURE

 NEW FEATURE

 NEW FEATURE

FrontPage's basic set of tools is extensive and will get the job done for just about all the basic tasks you need—creating pages, working with images, formatting text, making links, and coming up with innovative and interactive page layouts.

But when you take a step beyond the basics and consider the more advanced utilities and tools you can add to your FrontPage-based Web, you can quickly take your Web to a new level of professionalism. Without having to learn programming, you can achieve effects that used to be the sole province of Web masters and programmers.

First, there's a whole class of special effects that come under the heading of Dynamic HTML (DHTML for short). DHTML is a relatively new feature and isn't supported by older browsers, but if many of your visitors are likely to use the most recent versions of Web software, you can wow them by adding animation and transition effects to your pages.

Next, there's a set of advanced tools that become available to you when you select Web Component from the Insert menu. Web components are prepackaged programs you can add to a FrontPage-based Web to make it more functional and useful for your visitors. In this section, you'll learn how easy it is to add special effects and Web components to your site to enable your site to interact with visitors and give visitors a wider range of things they can do with your site.

Understanding DHTML

Dynamic HTML is a set of commands that enable Web pages to display animation in text, ads, images, marquees, buttons, and other Web page elements. Typically, a DHTML effect starts with an event that you specify and an object that the user will act on. Then you choose an effect from the first drop-down list in the DHTML Effects toolbar.

After you choose an event, you specify what should happen when the user performs the desired action. (The options vary depending on what event you specify.) Then you specify how you want the effect to take place. For instance, if you choose a Wipe effect for the Page Load event, you choose an option from the third drop-down list to describe how the page should wipe.

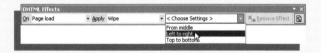

Enabling DHTML on Your Site

DHTML has the potential to bring many exciting effects to your FrontPage-based Web. You can create images that seem to bounce into place or fly in from the edge of the page, or you can create pages whose contents seem to come into focus gradually or that zoom in or out. First, though, you have to enable DHTML so you can begin to work with it.

Turn on DHTML

(1) Open the Web you want to work with.

(2) Choose Page Options from the Tools menu.

③ Click the Compatibility tab.

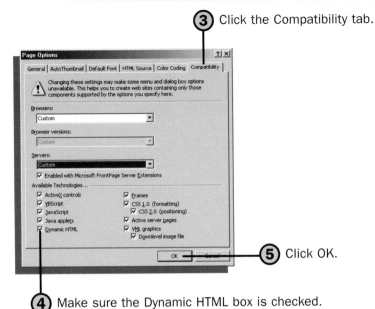

⑤ Click OK.

④ Make sure the Dynamic HTML box is checked.

Change DHTML Highlighting

By default, when working with DHTML Effects in Normal view, the affected area of the page is highlighted.

① Open the page you want to edit.

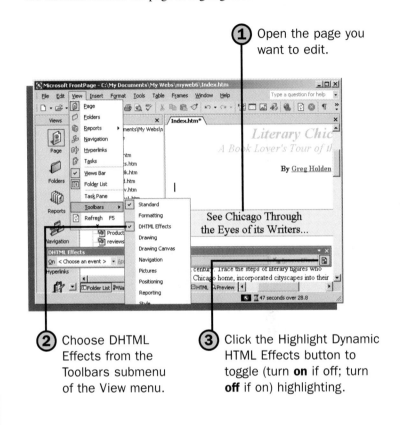

② Choose DHTML Effects from the Toolbars submenu of the View menu.

③ Click the Highlight Dynamic HTML Effects button to toggle (turn **on** if off; turn **off** if on) highlighting.

! TIP: You can choose an option from the Browser drop-down list to limit your page's functionality to a single type of Web browser. If you do this, however, bear in mind that you're limiting the number of users who can enjoy your site.

✋ CAUTION: If you have already formatted the current Web and added Dynamic HTML effects or Web components and you then change the status of the Dynamic HTML check box, some of the features on your Web might become unusable. It's best to enable or disable DHTML when you first begin to work with the Web.

✋ CAUTION: Blue highlighting of Dynamic HTML effects is for your benefit. It's not something your viewers see when they browse your Web. If you disable highlighting, your page might be easier to view but you might also lose track of elements you've formatted with DHTML. You might want to click the Preview tab to see how the page looks and works, without disabling the highlighting.

Creating a Page Transition

A page transition is a special effect that takes place when a viewer enters or leaves an individual page or a FrontPage-based Web. It's a flashy effect that lets your visitor know you've spent some time and effort in designing your site and that you take its contents seriously.

Specify the Transition Effect

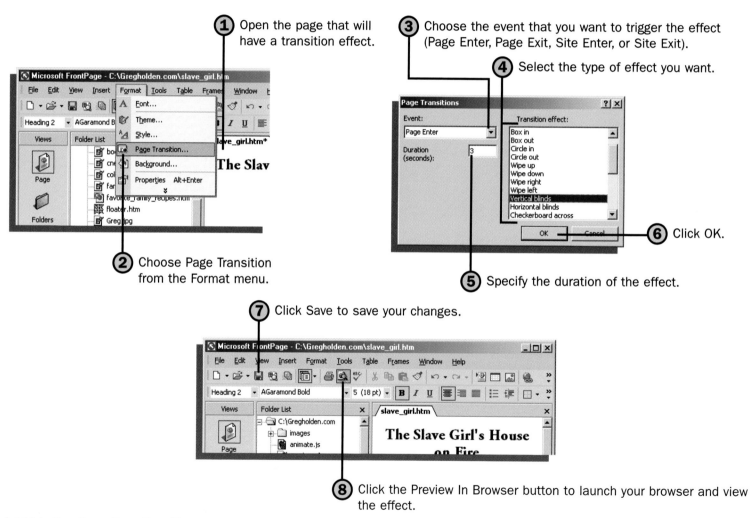

(1) Open the page that will have a transition effect.

(2) Choose Page Transition from the Format menu.

(3) Choose the event that you want to trigger the effect (Page Enter, Page Exit, Site Enter, or Site Exit).

(4) Select the type of effect you want.

(5) Specify the duration of the effect.

(6) Click OK.

(7) Click Save to save your changes.

(8) Click the Preview In Browser button to launch your browser and view the effect.

Change Transition Properties

(1) To change the transition, choose Page Transition from the Format menu again.

(2) Enter a new value (in seconds) for the duration of the effect.

(3) Choose a new transition effect.

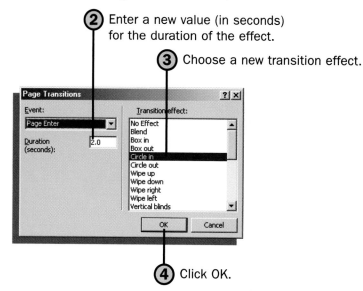

(4) Click OK.

Creating Text Rollovers

FrontPage can help you create a wide variety of text effects for your FrontPage-based Web. One of the most common is a rollover, an effect that occurs when the viewer passes the mouse pointer over an object. FrontPage makes it easy to specify rollover text—text whose formatting changes when the user passes the mouse over the text. (Not surprisingly, the trigger for this effect is called a *mouseover*.)

Define Font and Formatting

(1) Select the text you want to format.

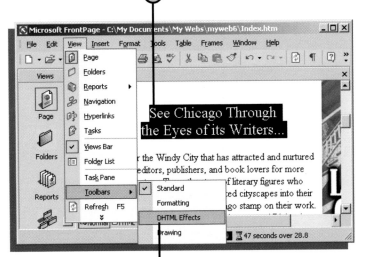

CAUTION: Text rollovers, like collapsible lists and other DHTML effects, aren't supported by all Web browsers. Viewers whose browsers don't support DHTML will just see the conventional list, text, or Web page without any special effects.

(2) Display the DHTML Effects toolbar by choosing DHTML Effects from the Toolbars submenu of the View menu.

(3) Select Mouse Over from the On drop-down list in the DHTML Effects toolbar.

(4) Select Formatting from the Apply drop-down list.

(5) Select Choose Font from the untitled drop-down list.

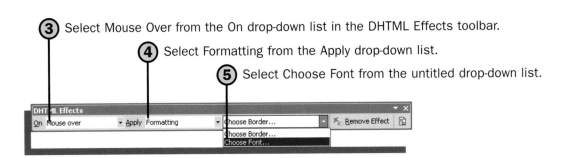

⑥ Select the font, style, point size, and color you want the text to appear in when the mouseover occurs.

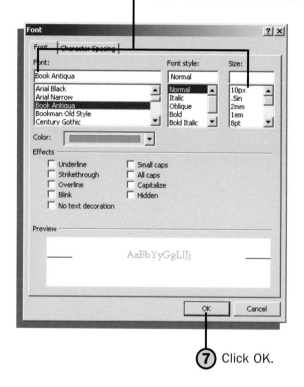

⑦ Click OK.

⑧ Click Preview.

⑨ Pass your mouse over the text to see the effect.

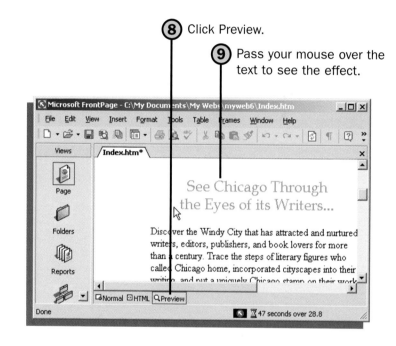

① **TIP:** The formatting that is applied when the mouse-over takes place should contrast with the normal formatting of the selected text. It's a good idea to make the text bold and in a different color, and possibly to choose a different font as well.

Adding DHTML Components

You can create some DHTML effects by adding them to your FrontPage-based Web as Web components. Web components automate many of the steps involved in creating animations or other features—many of which otherwise would require complex programming.

Add a Hover Button

① In an open Web page, position the cursor where you want a hover button to appear.

② Click the Web Component button.

③ Select Dynamic Effects in the Component Type list.

④ Select Hover Button in the Choose An Effect list.

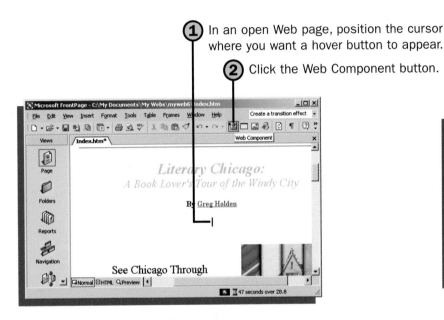

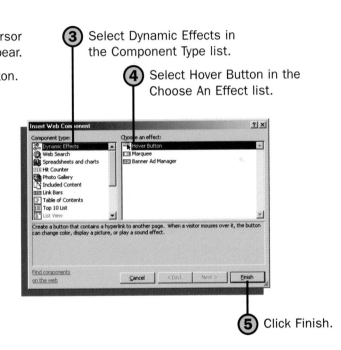

⑤ Click Finish.

!TIP: Your first choices don't have to be the be final ones. If you want to change a hover button's text, color, effect, or other properties, right-click the button and choose Hover Button Properties from the shortcut menu. You can then make your changes in the Hover Button Properties dialog box.

⑥ Set the button's properties, including where it should link, its color, and the animation effects.

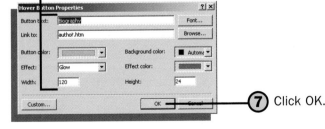

!TIP: To test the hover-button effect, click Save to save your changes and then Preview to preview the page. Pass the mouse pointer over the button to see how it changes.

⑦ Click OK.

Add a Banner Ad Manager

(1) Position the cursor at the location where you want the banner ad to appear.

(2) Click the Web Component button.

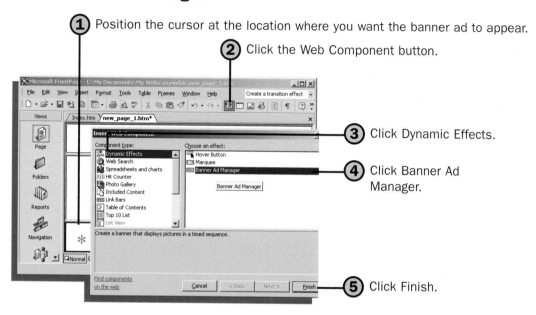

(3) Click Dynamic Effects.

(4) Click Banner Ad Manager.

(5) Click Finish.

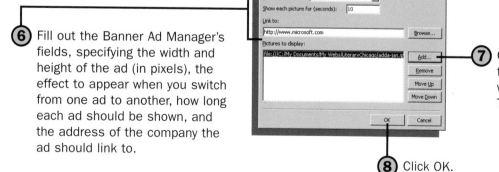

(6) Fill out the Banner Ad Manager's fields, specifying the width and height of the ad (in pixels), the effect to appear when you switch from one ad to another, how long each ad should be shown, and the address of the company the ad should link to.

(7) Click Add to locate the picture file on your computer or network and add it to the Pictures To Display list.

(8) Click OK.

Adding Search to a FrontPage-Based Web

The ability to search a Web site's contents by entering terms in a search form is one of the features most highly desired by Web surfers. Many visitors immediately turn to a search form to find something, rather than click on links. Normally, making a site searchable requires programming. FrontPage enables you to make your site searchable by inserting a Web component that indexes your site's contents and then searches the contents in response to search queries.

Choose a Web Search Component

① Open the Web you want to make searchable.

② Position the cursor at the spot where you want to insert the search form.

③ Click the Web Component button.

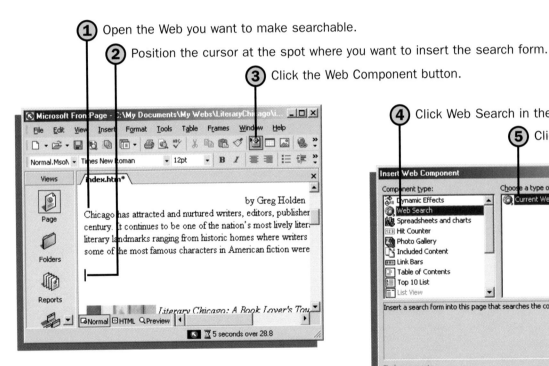

④ Click Web Search in the Component Type list.

⑤ Click Current Web.

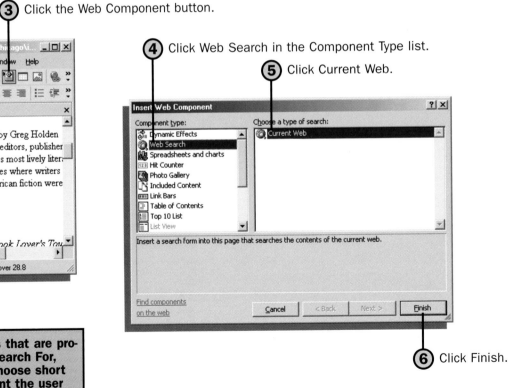

⑥ Click Finish.

> **! TIP:** If you replace the default labels that are provided for the search form, such as Search For, Start Search, and Reset, be sure to choose short labels that make it clear what you want the user to do when conducting a search.

Configure the Search Form

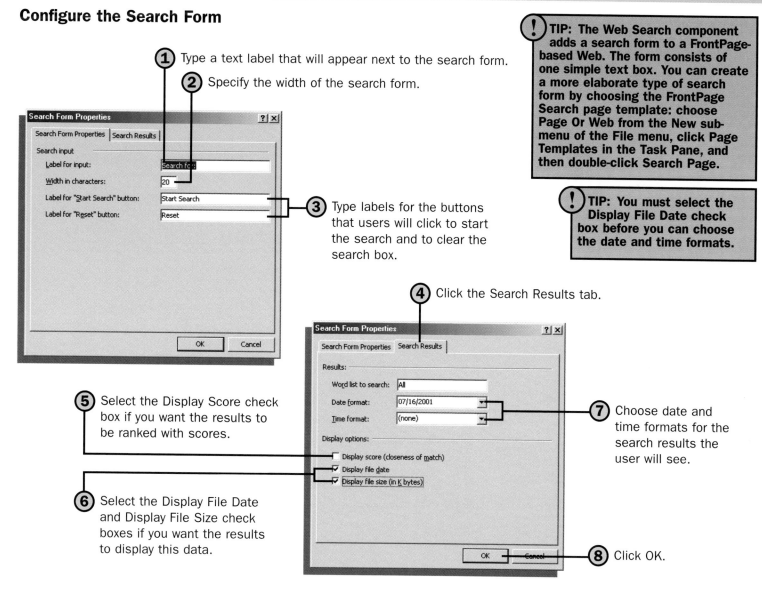

(1) Type a text label that will appear next to the search form.

(2) Specify the width of the search form.

TIP: The Web Search component adds a search form to a FrontPage-based Web. The form consists of one simple text box. You can create a more elaborate type of search form by choosing the FrontPage Search page template: choose Page Or Web from the New submenu of the File menu, click Page Templates in the Task Pane, and then double-click Search Page.

TIP: You must select the Display File Date check box before you can choose the date and time formats.

(3) Type labels for the buttons that users will click to start the search and to clear the search box.

(4) Click the Search Results tab.

(5) Select the Display Score check box if you want the results to be ranked with scores.

(6) Select the Display File Date and Display File Size check boxes if you want the results to display this data.

(7) Choose date and time formats for the search results the user will see.

(8) Click OK.

Including Microsoft Excel Components

Some of the FrontPage Web components enable you to include Microsoft Excel spreadsheets and other documents in your FrontPage-based Web. Your visitors can directly interact with the data contained in the documents. By embedding a spreadsheet or a chart in a Web page, companies can make data available to employees without requiring them to install the original applications—the Web browser becomes a uniform interface to access databases, spreadsheets, charts, and many other types of information.

Add an Office Spreadsheet

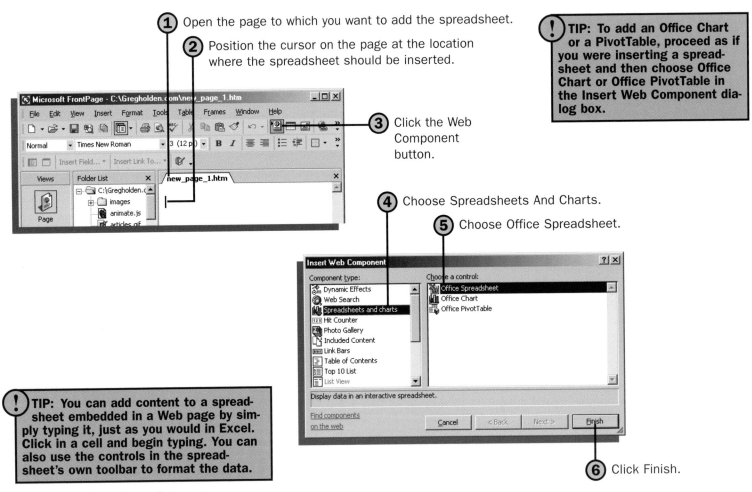

(1) Open the page to which you want to add the spreadsheet.

(2) Position the cursor on the page at the location where the spreadsheet should be inserted.

(3) Click the Web Component button.

TIP: To add an Office Chart or a PivotTable, proceed as if you were inserting a spreadsheet and then choose Office Chart or Office PivotTable in the Insert Web Component dialog box.

(4) Choose Spreadsheets And Charts.

(5) Choose Office Spreadsheet.

TIP: You can add content to a spreadsheet embedded in a Web page by simply typing it, just as you would in Excel. Click in a cell and begin typing. You can also use the controls in the spreadsheet's own toolbar to format the data.

(6) Click Finish.

Import Data into an Office Spreadsheet

① To import data from a file, click the spreadsheet to make it active and then click Commands And Options on the Office spreadsheet's toolbar.

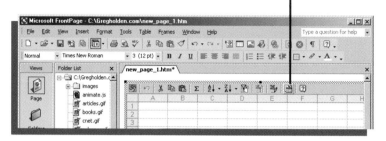

② Click the Import tab.

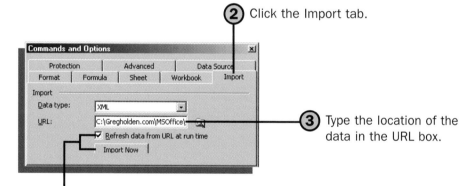

TIP: You can link your spreadsheet to a data source by clicking Commands And Options and then clicking the Data Source tab in the Commands And Options dialog box. Enter the URL of the sheet data source in the Connection box.

③ Type the location of the data in the URL box.

④ If you want to update your data whenever the spreadsheet loads, check Refresh Data From URL At Run Time. Otherwise, click Import Now.

CAUTION: Don't expect all your visitors to be able to interact with spreadsheets or other Office Web components. In order to use the interactive data, they need to use Internet Explorer 4.01 or later, and have Microsoft Office Web components installed, available either as part of a site license for Microsoft Office XP or directly as a component of the individually packaged Microsoft Office XP.

CAUTION: The normal Excel file format (.XSL) cannot be imported. You must save the Excel spreadsheet in XML, HTML, or CSV format and then import the file in that format. Any of these three formats will allow you to view the spreadsheet, but only the XML and HTML formats allow you to modify the data in the spreadsheet and immediately see the results of changes. None of these formats, however, allow you to save your changes to the spreadsheet.

Counting Visitors

Hit counters are popular with Web site owners and visitors alike. A hit counter is a utility that records the number of visits that are made to a Web page. They give visitors and site owners an idea of how much traffic a page is generating. FrontPage lets you add a counter to any page in the form of a Web component.

Add a Hit Counter

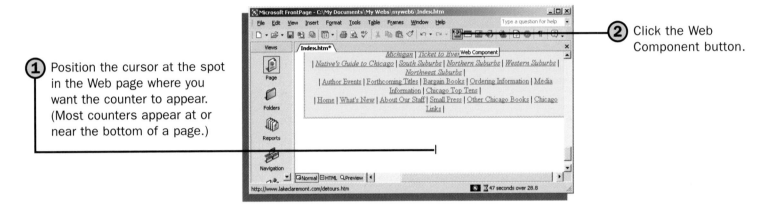

① Position the cursor at the spot in the Web page where you want the counter to appear. (Most counters appear at or near the bottom of a page.)

② Click the Web Component button.

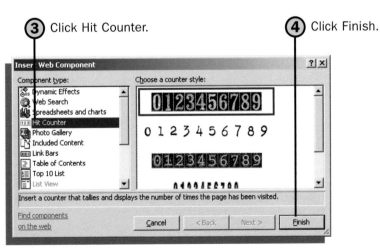

③ Click Hit Counter.

④ Click Finish.

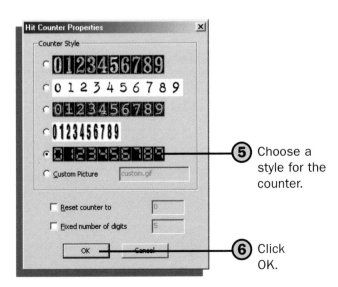

⑤ Choose a style for the counter.

⑥ Click OK.

Adjust a Hit Counter

(1) Right-click [Hit Counter].

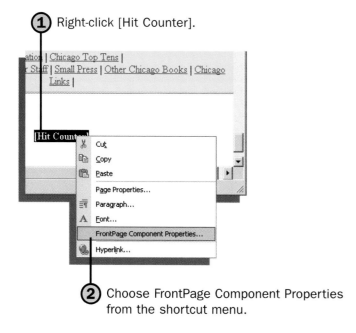

(2) Choose FrontPage Component Properties from the shortcut menu.

(3) Set the hit counter properties, including the counter style, the number of digits, the number to start counting from, and a custom GIF image if you'd like to use that to display the digits.

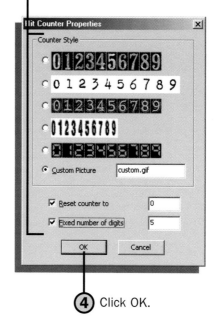

(4) Click OK.

SEE ALSO: If you sign up to use the Microsoft Web hosting service, bCentral, you get free access to a utility called FastCounter that you can use to track visitors to your Web site. For more details, see "Using bCentral Web Components" on page 166.

TIP: You can't test your hit counter until your Web page is published on a Web server. Once it is published, click the Preview In Browser button to test it. In order for the counter to work, the server has to have the FrontPage Server Extensions installed on it. Check with your network administrator or ISP to see if the extensions are installed.

CAUTION: Hit counters are not a perfectly accurate representation of how many unique visits you're getting to a page. Counters also record visits you make to the page to test and edit it, and they record visits by search engine programs that index Web pages to add them to their databases. Use your hit counter as a rough estimate of the number of visits, not as an exact count.

Showing Photographs ⊛ NEW FEATURE

If you want to use the same graphic elements consistently on your Web pages and need a place to organize and present those images, you can use a new feature called the Photo Gallery. Once you've assembled logos and other images you expect to reuse regularly, you can use the FrontPage Insert menu to create and access your gallery. Photo Gallery even lets you add captions and descriptions to your images.

Add a Photo Gallery

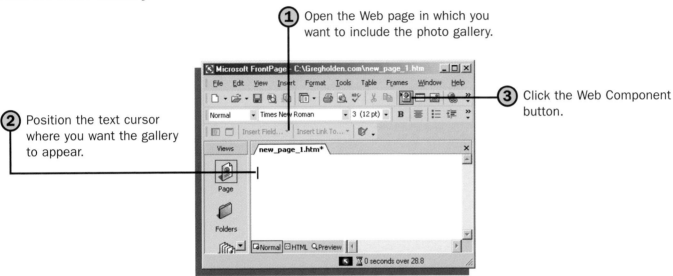

(1) Open the Web page in which you want to include the photo gallery.

(2) Position the text cursor where you want the gallery to appear.

(3) Click the Web Component button.

TRY THIS! You can add photos directly from a scanner or a digital camera as well as from files on your computer or network. When you click the Add button in the Photo Gallery Properties dialog box, a drop-down menu appears. Choose Pictures From Scanner Or Cameras. In the Insert Picture From Scanner Or Camera dialog box, specify the image input device you want to use. Then click Insert or Custom Insert to connect to the device so you can select images.

TIP: Once you add a photo gallery, you can format it as you would any other Web page. You can assign a theme to the page to correspond to other pages in your Web site, for instance.

④ Select Photo Gallery.

⑤ Select the photo gallery layout you want to use.

TRY THIS! You can customize a gallery's layout by right-clicking it and choosing Photo Gallery Properties from the shortcut menu that appears. On the layout tab, you can select a layout and set the number of photos that will appear in each row.

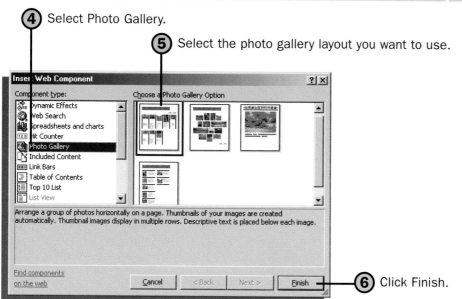

⑥ Click Finish.

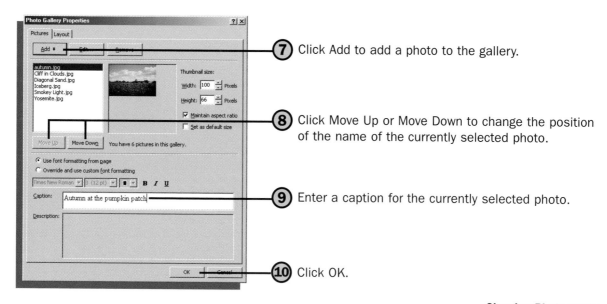

⑦ Click Add to add a photo to the gallery.

⑧ Click Move Up or Move Down to change the position of the name of the currently selected photo.

⑨ Enter a caption for the currently selected photo.

⑩ Click OK.

Using Included Content Components

Maintaining a Web site can be time-consuming, and it's to your advantage to automate some of the processes that involve adding and displaying content. The FrontPage Web components help you automate several tasks. You can insert standard information such as the page author's name in multiple pages, and you can create standard headers and footers that FrontPage will insert into existing pages.

Substitute Content

① Open the Web in which you want to include standardized content.

② Position the cursor where you want to add the content.

③ Click the Web Component button.

④ Select Included Content.

⑤ Select Substitution.

⑥ Click Finish.

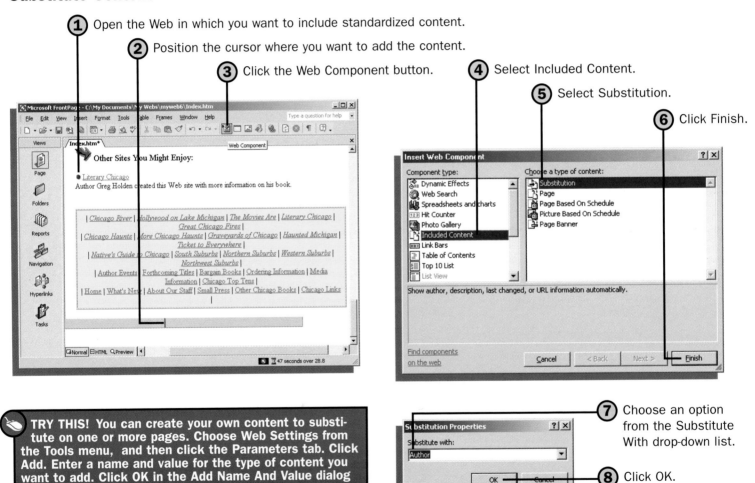

⑦ Choose an option from the Substitute With drop-down list.

⑧ Click OK.

TRY THIS! You can create your own content to substitute on one or more pages. Choose Web Settings from the Tools menu, and then click the Parameters tab. Click Add. Enter a name and value for the type of content you want to add. Click OK in the Add Name And Value dialog box, and then click OK in the Web Settings dialog box.

Add an Included Page

① Position the cursor at the location where you want the included page information to appear, and click the Web Component button.

② Click Included Content and then Page.

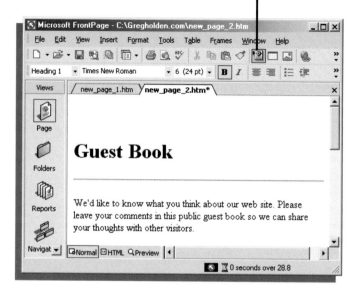

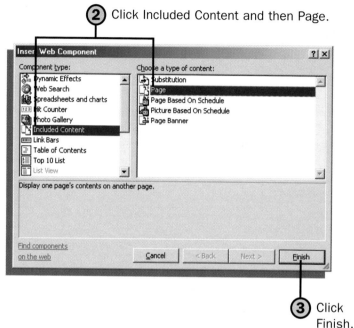

③ Click Finish.

④ Enter the URL for the page you want to include in the Page To Include box, or click Browse to locate the file on your computer or network.

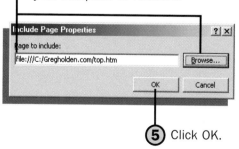

⑤ Click OK.

! TIP: If you want to add the included page's contents as a footer to the currently displayed Web page, position the cursor at the bottom of the current page before you click the Web Component button. If you want to add the included page as a header, position the cursor at the top of the page.

! TIP: You can use the Include Page component to add a page from another Web site, such as a search engine page; just enter the page's URL in the Page To Include box in the Include Page Properties dialog box. Be careful, though, that you do not infringe on a copyright in doing so.

Adding an Expedia Component

It's often useful to provide visitors with maps to an event—or, if you're designing a business site, a map to your office. You can do it by adding an Expedia Web component to your site. You can either add a link to a map on the Expedia Web site, or add a map of a specific location.

Add a Map

(1) Position the cursor where you want the map to appear.

(2) Click the Web Component button.

(3) Click Expedia Components.

(4) Click Static Map.

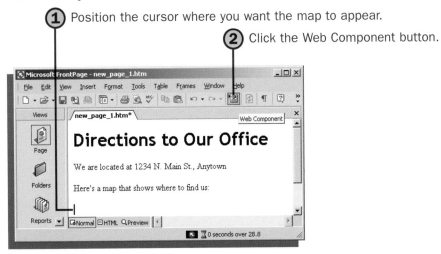

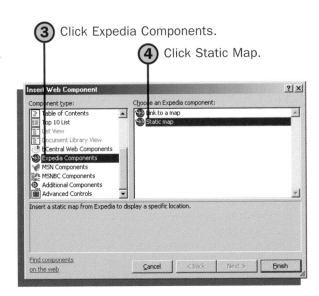

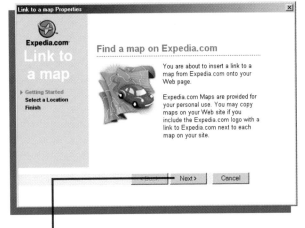

(5) Click Next, and follow the wizard through subsequent steps to add the map to your page.

> **(!) TIP: You will see only a placeholder icon in Normal view. To see your map, select the Preview view or click the Preview In Browser button on the toolbar.**

> **TRY THIS! You can also add a link to a map instead of an actual map. Click the Web Component button, click Expedia Components, and click Link To A Map. Click Finish, and follow the wizard through the process of adding the map link. The advantage of doing this is that the link takes the viewer to live information on the Expedia Web site. When you add an actual map, the map is static—it never changes after you insert the map (unless, of course, you replace it at some point).**

Using MSN and MSNBC Components ⊛ NEW FEATURE

News headlines are among the most popular types of content included on the home pages of many Web sites. So are search utilities that let visitors instantly search the entire Web from your site. By providing your visitors with the latest news, you give them another reason to remain on your site instead of going elsewhere. FrontPage gives you the ability to insert live news headlines from MSN and MSNBC— the information is gathered fresh from these news services whenever the viewer's browser accesses the page.

Add an MSN Component

① Open the page that you want to include the MSN component.

② Position the cursor where you want the headlines to appear.

③ Click the Web Component button.

④ Click MSN Components.

⑤ Click the MSN component you want to add.

⑥ Click Finish.

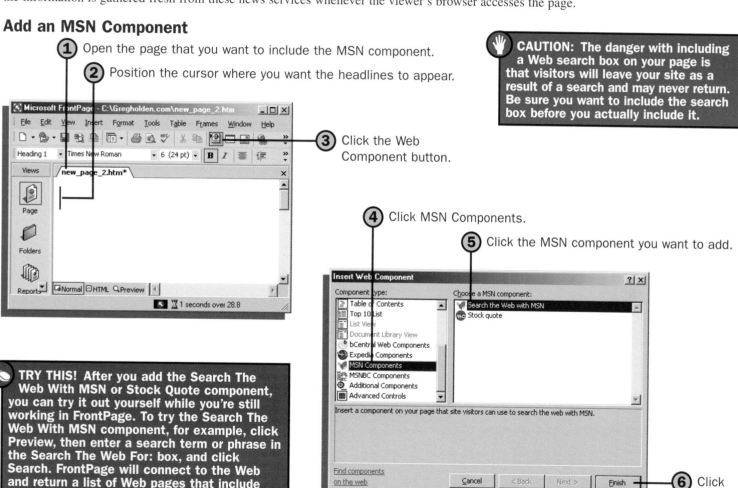

CAUTION: The danger with including a Web search box on your page is that visitors will leave your site as a result of a search and may never return. Be sure you want to include the search box before you actually include it.

TRY THIS! After you add the Search The Web With MSN or Stock Quote component, you can try it out yourself while you're still working in FrontPage. To try the Search The Web With MSN component, for example, click Preview, then enter a search term or phrase in the Search The Web For: box, and click Search. FrontPage will connect to the Web and return a list of Web pages that include the terms.

Add an MSNBC Component

(1) Position the cursor on the Web page where you want the MSNBC component to appear.

(2) Click the Web Component button.

(3) Click MSNBC Components.

(4) Click the type of MSNBC content you want to add.

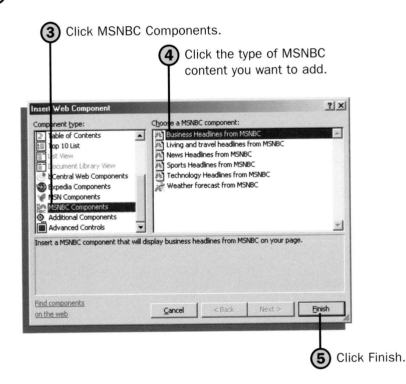

(5) Click Finish.

CAUTION: Adding live headlines from MSNBC will make your page load slower, since users will have to wait for the information to be delivered from MSNBC.com. Don't add dynamic content just because you can; it should add something important to your page.

Adding SharePoint Components ⊛ NEW FEATURE

Microsoft SharePoint is Web server software that enables workgroups to collaborate and share information. If your office or workgroup has a server running SharePoint, you can use FrontPage to generate interactive elements that your colleagues can use to enter information. You can create an interactive list in which users can enter data, such as a sign-up sheet; you can also create a view of a document library where users can store files.

Add a List View

① Open the page that you want to contain a view of an interactive list.

② Position the cursor where you want the list view to appear.

③ Click the Web Component button.

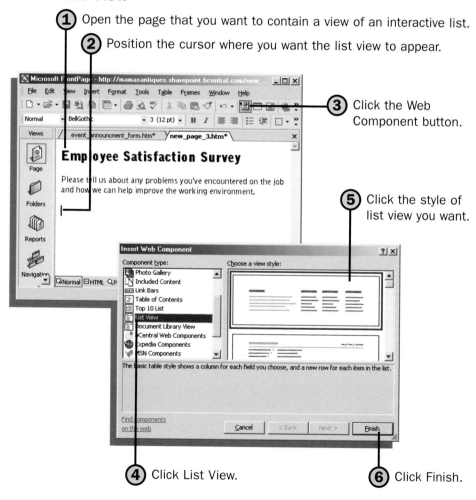

⑤ Click the style of list view you want.

④ Click List View.

⑥ Click Finish.

⑦ Click the list or survey you want.

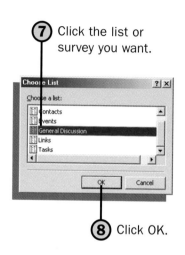

⑧ Click OK.

⑨ Modify the fields or other properties you want the list to contain.

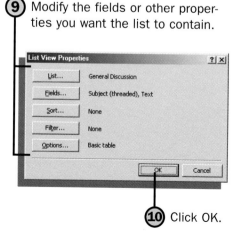

⑩ Click OK.

Add a Document Library View

① Position the cursor where you want the list view to appear.

② Click the Web Component button.

③ Click Document Library View.

④ Click the layout that you want the view to have.

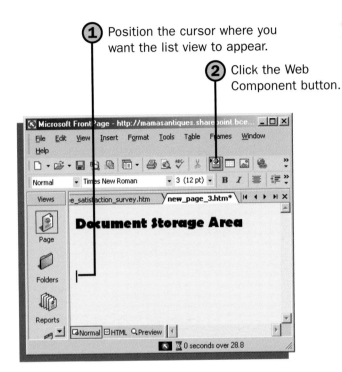

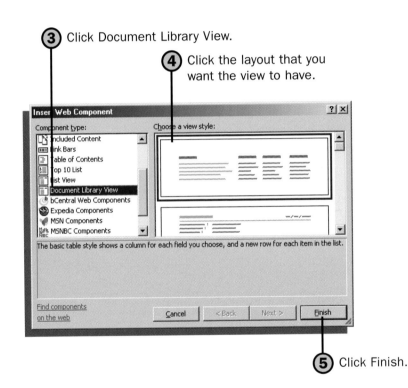

⑤ Click Finish.

! TIP: If you don't want to set up SharePoint on your own computer, you can sign up for an account with bCentral or another Web hosting service that runs SharePoint. You'll find a list of SharePoint hosting services at *www.microsoft.com/ frontpage/sharepoint/WPP.htm*.

6 Click the Document Library you want to add.

Choose Document Library dialog box

Choose a document library:

Shared Documents

OK   Cancel

7 Click OK.

CAUTION: In order to add a view of an interactive list or document library to a Web page, the page must be on the same Web site as the list or document library itself, and the Web site must be on a server that is running Microsoft SharePoint. You can't create the list or library view on a site that exists only on your local computer: the List view and Document Library view options won't be activated in the Insert Web Component dialog box, so you won't be able to select them.

8 Click Fields to add fields to the library.

Document Library View Properties dialog box

Library...	Shared Documents
Fields...	Document Icon, File Name (linked to document), Edit
Sort...	None
Filter...	None
Options...	Basic table

OK   Cancel

9 Choose one or more fields from the Available Fields list, and then click Add.

Displayed Fields dialog box

Choose the fields to display.

Available fields:

Created Date
Document Created E
Document Modified E
File Name
File Name (no path)
File Size
ID
Title

Add >>
<< Remove
Move Up
Move Down

Displayed fields:

Document Icon
File Name (linked to
Edit (link to edit item
Last Modified
Modified By

OK   Cancel

10 Click OK.

Using bCentral Web Components

The Microsoft bCentral Web hosting site provides extensive resources for individuals who want to start their own online businesses. Among the advantages of choosing bCentral as your host are the utilities that help make your business site more useful for your prospective customers. bCentral gives its customers access to a variety of Web site add-ons, two of which (a hit counter and a link exchange system) are made available to FrontPage users as Web components you can add to your own site—whether you're on bCentral or not.

Add a Counter

(1) In an open page, position the cursor at the location where you want the counter to appear.

(2) Click the Web Component button.

> **TIP:** In order to use the bCentral FastCounter you need to sign up for a free account with bCentral, as explained in the FastCounter Properties wizard.

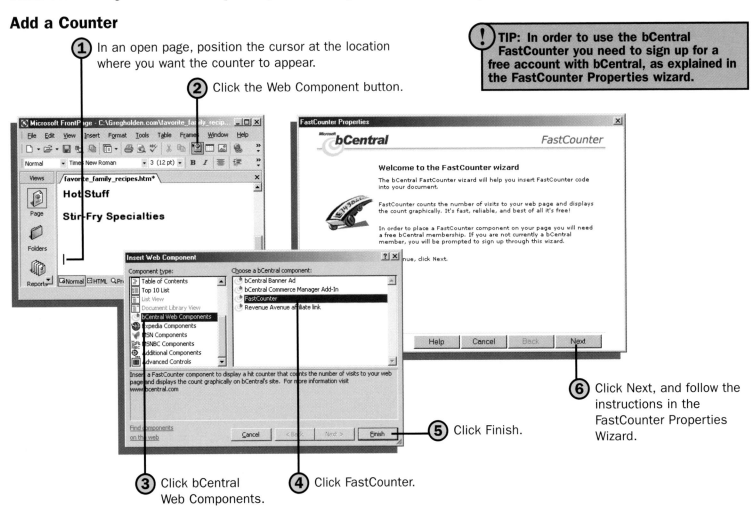

(3) Click bCentral Web Components.

(4) Click FastCounter.

(5) Click Finish.

(6) Click Next, and follow the instructions in the FastCounter Properties Wizard.

Add a Revenue Source

① Position the cursor on the page where you want the link to appear.

② Click the Web Component button.

③ Click bCentral Web Components.

④ Click Revenue Avenue Affiliate Link.

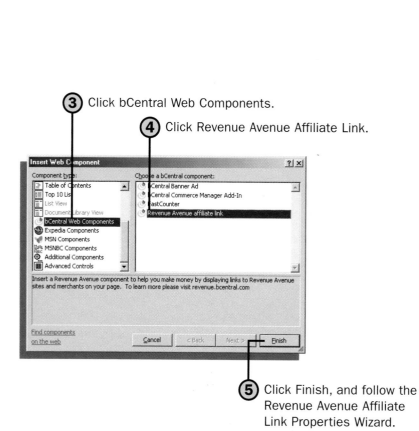

⑤ Click Finish, and follow the Revenue Avenue Affiliate Link Properties Wizard.

10 Working with Forms

❄ NEW FEATURE

Forms add a new level of interactivity to a Web site, turning it into a two-way communication medium. Usually Web surfers find out about you when they visit your site; you don't learn too much about who they are unless you give them a form to fill out.

The ability to help users create forms that actually work has always been one of FrontPage's strongest features. FrontPage not only streamlines the process of creating the data entry part of a form—the text boxes, buttons, and other elements that the user fills out—but it also provides the computer programs that process the information someone sends you and presents it in a form you can read and use, such as an e-mail message.

Creating an effective Web page form is a balancing act. You want the form to be easy for your users to fill out. But you also want the information to be useful to you, and you want to control how users fill out the form so that they give you the information you are looking for. FrontPage can help you strike a balance between giving users freedom and setting rules so that they fill out the form the way you want them to.

In this section, you will learn how forms work and about the individual elements that the user sees. You'll learn about the different options for creating forms. First you'll learn how to use the shortcut methods, the templates and wizards. You'll get detailed instructions on creating individual parts of a form. Then you'll learn how to control the way user information is sent to you.

Creating a Form

Web page forms are commonly used to register visitors for services or to give them a chance to voice their opinions. Common Web page forms include a guest book, where visitors can post their names and comments on a Web page, and feedback forms, where visitors can submit their comments to the Web site owner. FrontPage gives you templates that enable you to create both forms instantly without having to create each data entry element from scratch; your job is to customize the contents with your own content.

Use the Wizard or a Template

(1) With a page open, choose Page Or Web from the New submenu of the File menu.

(2) Click Page Templates in the New From Template section of the Task Pane.

(3) Do one of the following:

- Double-click Form Page Wizard to open it. The wizard will step you through the options in a form, allowing you to define the question or prompt that the user will see, the type of information to be gathered, and how the information is to be sent to you.

- Click one of the two form templates in the Page Templates dialog box (Guest Book or Feedback Form).

(4) Click OK.

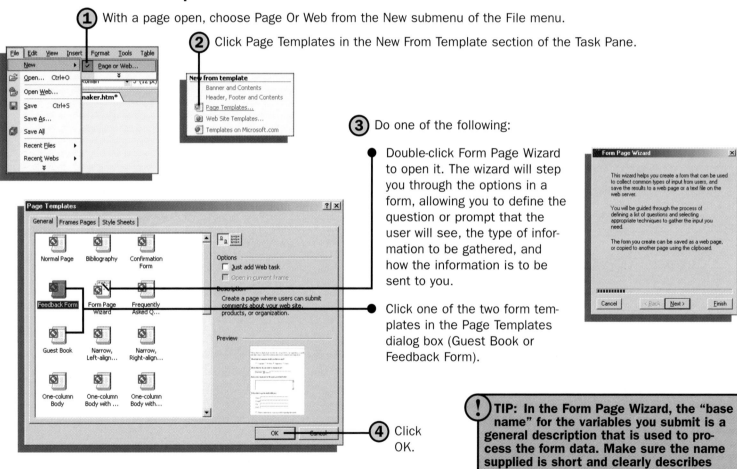

! TIP: In the Form Page Wizard, the "base name" for the variables you submit is a general description that is used to process the form data. Make sure the name supplied is short and clearly describes the data entry elements you're using.

CAUTION: Limit the personal information you want the user to submit. Many surfers are put off by forms that ask them to reveal a lot about their personal lives. Some may skip filling out your form altogether if they feel their privacy is being invaded.

TIP: The term "CGI script," which appears on one of the wizard screens, refers to a program that uses the Common Gateway Interface (CGI), a way for Web servers and client programs to communicate with one another.

5 When the page appears, select the placeholder text and replace it with your own content.

TIP: Once your Web form has been published to a Web server running SharePoint or the FrontPage Server Extensions, you can test the form yourself by clicking Preview In Browser.

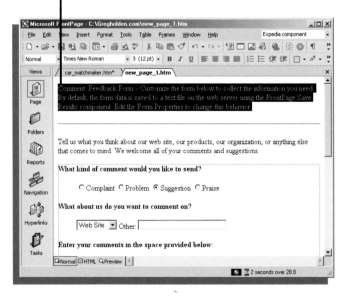

CAUTION: Unless you use a custom script (a computer program written in a language such as Perl or C++) to process the information submitted from a Web page form when it is sent to your Web server, you need to have the FrontPage Server Extensions or Microsoft SharePoint running on the server that hosts your site. Otherwise you won't be able to use a FrontPage form handler to process the information that comes to you from a Web page form. Ask your Internet Service Provider or network administrator whether SharePoint or the server extensions are available.

Using List Forms ⊛ NEW FEATURE

A list form is a form that enables members of a workgroup to share ideas and submit information. List forms are part of SharePoint Team Services. List forms require that the page that contains the form be published on a server that is running Microsoft SharePoint. A list form, like other Web page forms, contains one or more fields, which are data entry elements that give the user a place to enter information.

Add a List Form

① With a page open, choose List Form from the Form submenu of the Insert menu.

! TIP: The List Or Document Library To Use For Form drop-down list in the List Or Document Library Form dialog box lets you choose from the following types of list forms: Announcements, Contact, Events, General Discussion, Links, Shared Documents, and Tasks.

! TIP: Each Web page can contain no more than one list form.

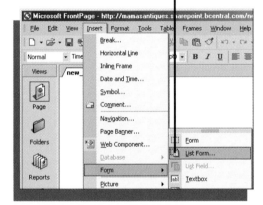

④ Click Save to name and save your page on the SharePoint server.

② Select New Item Form if you want visitors to add items to the list form, Edit Item Form if you want visitors to be able to edit items in the list or to change their own responses, or Display Item Form if you want visitors to be able to view responses to a survey.

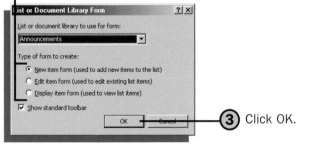

③ Click OK.

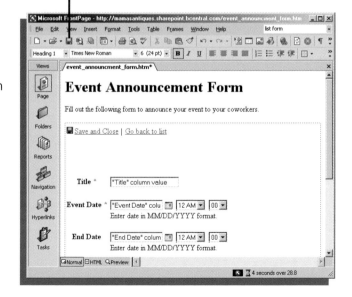

Add List Fields

(1) Right-click the list form.

(2) Choose Layout Customization View from the shortcut menu.

(3) Once the form has changed to layout customization view, right-click anywhere in the form and choose List Field from the shortcut menu.

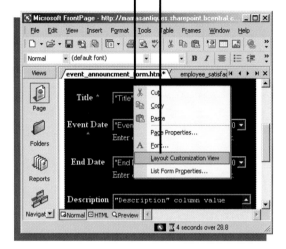

(4) Choose the field you want to add from the Field To Display drop down list.

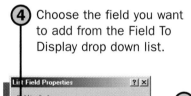

(5) Specify whether you want to show only the name of the field or the field data—in other words, the contents of the field.

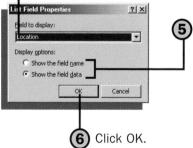

(6) Click OK.

✓ **SEE ALSO: For more information about creating interactive lists and document libraries, see "Adding SharePoint Components" on page 163.**

Delete a List Field

① Single-click the field you want to remove.

② Click the
Cut button.

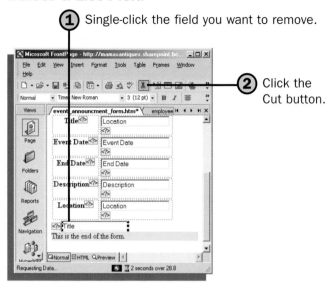

> ! **TIP:** To change the order of the fields in the list form, click the field you want to move and drag it to a new location.

> ✋ **CAUTION:** If you want to add a new field to your list form, don't right-click an existing field when you choose List Field. If you do, you'll replace the existing field with a new one. Instead, right-click a part of the form that doesn't yet contain a field.

> ! **TIP:** When you first create a list form, FrontPage displays it in Live Data view. The List Field option doesn't appear when you right-click the form in this view, however. You need to switch to Layout Customization view first.

Adding Text Boxes and Areas

The text box that enables the user to enter a single line of text is probably the single most common data entry element used in Web page forms. Whether you're creating your own form from scratch or editing an existing form, FrontPage makes it easy to create the box and control its size.

Insert a Text Box

① Enter text for your form and format it as you would any other text.

② Enter a label for the text box you want to create, and press the spacebar once or twice.

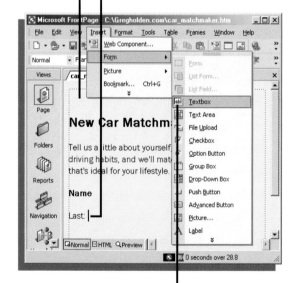

③ Choose Textbox from the Form submenu of the Insert menu.

Insert a Text Area

① Position the cursor at the location in the form where you want the text area (a scrolling text box) to appear.

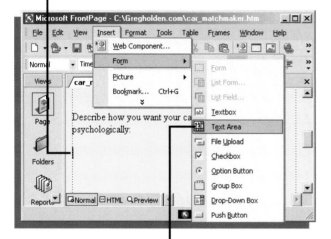

② Choose Text Area from the Form submenu of the Insert menu.

ⓘ TIP: The Name field, in both the Text Box Properties dialog box and in the TextArea Box Properties dialog box, becomes important when you receive and process the information you receive from the form. The data entered in the box will be presented next to the box's name, in a form such as "Lastname=Holden". Make sure the Name box contains a clear indication of the field's contents so that you can process the information more easily.

Avoiding Bad Form: Get Your Visitors to Talk Back

Forms are a critical part of a business Web site. E-commerce depends on getting shoppers to fill out forms to register, make purchases, or specify shipping and billing information. Yet, many forms actually turn shoppers away because they are poorly designed and difficult to fill out. By following some simple rules of thumb you can turn your form from a head-scratcher into a no-brainer:

● Give your users enough space in which to type. Most street addresses (and a few proper names) need more than the 20 characters contained in FrontPage's default text box. Drag the box's right edge to provide more room.

● Keep your forms organized. Arrange the form fields in a logical order—first the name, then the address, then the phone number and e-mail address, and so on. You might want to sketch the form out on a sheet of paper to help organize your thoughts.

● Don't leave your visitors guessing. Spell out which fields are required and which are optional. Highlight the names of required fields in a color or mark them with an asterisk.

● Protect secure information. If you want visitors to type a password in a field, click Yes next to Password Field in the Text Box Properties dialog box when you create that field. FrontPage configures the box so that a Web browser will display only asterisks rather than characters or numbers when someone types a password.

Forms communicate something about your organization. A bad experience filling out a form can turn your visitors off. If you take a few minutes to organize your forms and make them user-friendly, you'll get better responses.

Adding Drop-Down Boxes

If you want to give your visitors the chance to choose one option from a group of options while enabling them to scroll through a list of possible responses, create a drop-down box. Drop-down boxes are ideal for long lists—the obvious example is a list of all 50 states in the U.S. from which the user has to make a selection.

Insert a Drop-Down Box

(1) Position the cursor at the location in the form where you want the drop-down box to appear.

(2) Select Drop-Down Box from the Form submenu of the Insert menu.

(3) Right-click the drop-down box, and then choose Form Field Properties from the shortcut menu.

(5) Click Add. (For each item you want to include in the list, you need to click Add and then follow steps 6 through 8 below.)

(6) In the Choice box in the Add Choice dialog box, type the name of the first item you want to list.

(4) Type a short but descriptive name for the drop-down menu in the Name box.

(7) Check Selected if you want the list item to be selected initially.

(8) Click OK.

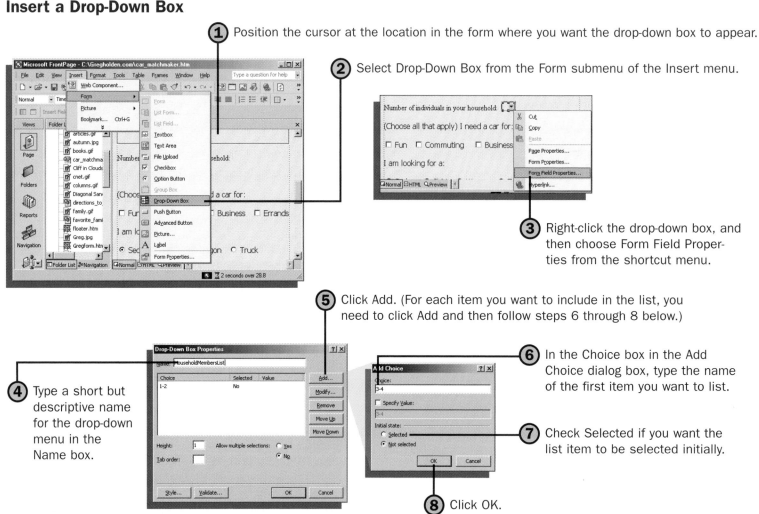

Adding Buttons

When users have finished filling out your form, they need to submit the information to you. Clicking the Submit button sends the user information to the form handler that has been associated with the form so that you can receive the data and make use of it. Clicking Reset tells the user's browser to reset the buttons to their original values. You can use either a push button or an advanced button to place Submit and Reset buttons where you prefer.

Add a Push Button

1 Position the cursor in the form where you want the button to appear.

2 Choose Push Button from the Form submenu of the Insert menu.

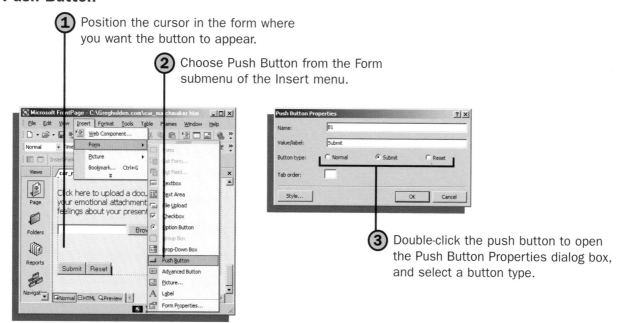

3 Double-click the push button to open the Push Button Properties dialog box, and select a button type.

TRY THIS: By default, the Submit and Reset buttons that FrontPage inserts when you create a form are immediately next to one another with no spaces between them. You can click to position the cursor and add a space or two between them so that users don't mistakenly click Reset instead of Submit.

Add an Advanced Button

1 With the cursor positioned at the location in the form where you want to add an advanced button, choose Advanced Button from the Form submenu of the Insert menu.

2 Right-click the advanced button, select Advanced Button Properties from the shortcut menu, and then select a button type.

3 Type a name for your button.

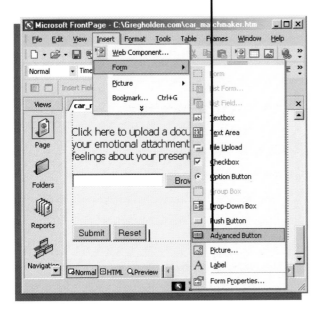

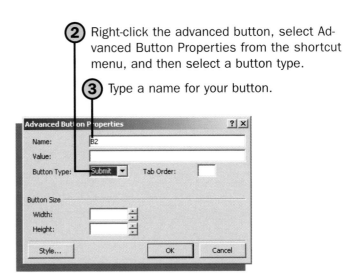

> **!TIP:** Some forms don't require a Reset button. You can delete it by selecting it and then pressing the DELETE key.

> **!TIP:** There's no reason why the buttons have to bear the generic labels Submit and Reset. You can change the labels to anything you want. Right-click the button, choose Form Field Properties from the shortcut menu, and replace the current label in the Value/Label box with your own label.

Adding Check Boxes and Option Buttons

Many Web page forms give users the ability to choose one or more selections from a group of options by clicking on boxes or option buttons. Such boxes help users along by providing them with possible selections. Check boxes give users the ability to select more than one option, or even all the options, while option buttons enable users to select only one choice from a group.

Add a Check Box or an Option Button

(1) Position the cursor at the spot in the form where you want the box to appear.

(2) Choose Checkbox or Option Button from the Form submenu of the Insert menu.

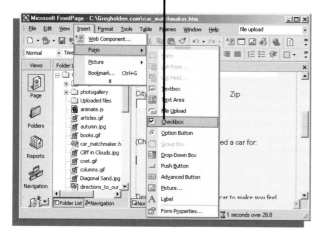

(3) Type a label for the box or button.

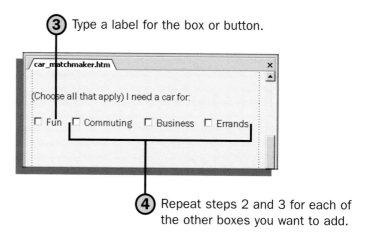

(4) Repeat steps 2 and 3 for each of the other boxes you want to add.

> **TRY THIS:** If you think one of the choices in a group of option buttons or check boxes is likely to be selected more often than the others, you can set its Initial State to selected. Right-click the button or box, and then choose Form Field Properties from the shortcut menu.

Adding Hidden Fields

A hidden field is something the user doesn't actually see when filling out the form you've created. Sometimes hidden fields are essential and provide information that a script, a database, or a file needs to process the form information. Otherwise, a hidden field is like a note to yourself that you see when you receive the data from the file. When you create a hidden field, you can include information about the name of the form, the place it was published, or the version number of the form.

Add a Hidden Field

1 Right-click anywhere in the form, and then choose Form Properties from the shortcut menu.

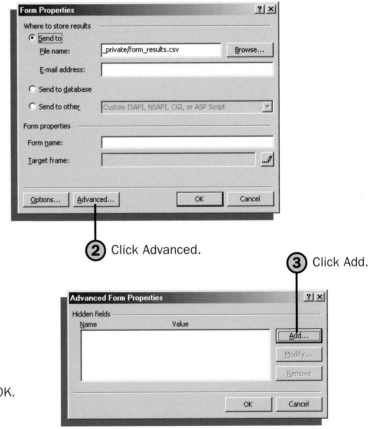

2 Click Advanced.

3 Click Add.

4 Enter a name and a value for the hidden field, and then click OK.

Storing Form Results

Simply creating a form's public face is one thing, but the next phase is equally important—you need to tell FrontPage what should happen with the data that the form collects. For some forms, you'll want to save the results to a file in your FrontPage-based Web so you can work with them later. If the data you're collecting is short, you can also have the results sent to you in the form of an e-mail message.

Save Form Results in a File

(1) Right-click anywhere in the form.

(2) Choose Form Properties from the shortcut menu.

(3) To send the results to a file on your Web site, click Send To.

(4) Enter a new file name or folder name, or click Browse to locate a folder on your Web site where you want to store the results.

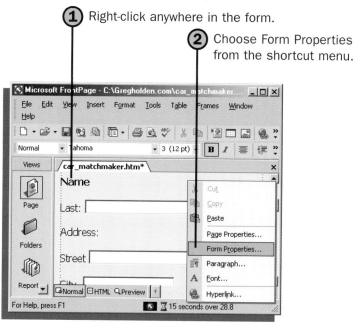

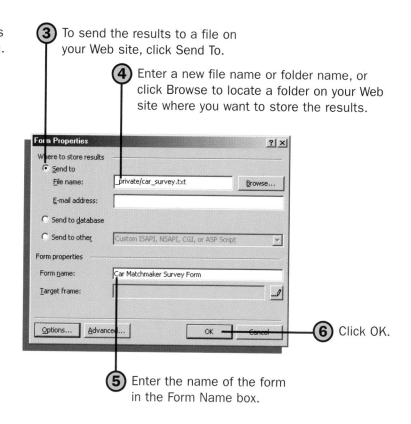

(6) Click OK.

(5) Enter the name of the form in the Form Name box.

! TIP: It's a good idea to change the default form results file name (form_results) to something more specific, so you know exactly what the file contains when you want to view it.

E-Mail Form Results

① Right-click anywhere in the form.

② Choose Form Properties from the shortcut menu.

③ Click Send To.

④ Enter the e-mail address where you want the form results to be sent.

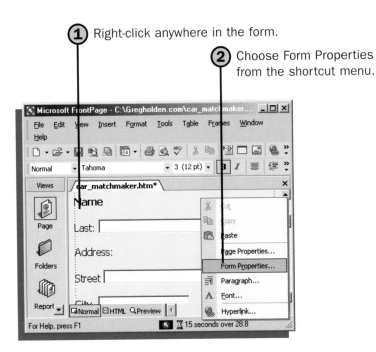

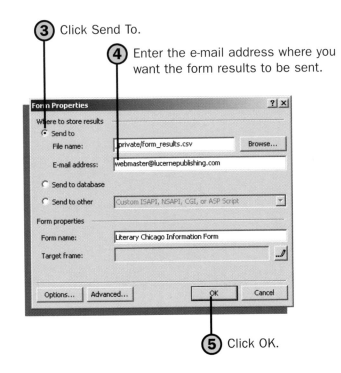

⑤ Click OK.

!TIP: The utility that processes your form results is called a form handler—a program that runs on the Web server that hosts your site. When FrontPage creates the form, it identifies the form handler that needs to run when the data is sent to the server.

!TIP: Be sure to test your form and the form handler before you open your Web site to the public. You should be the first one to fill out the form and send yourself some test results so that you see if the form handler works correctly.

✋CAUTION: The form results are sent, by default, to the folder _private on your Web. This folder cannot be browsed by your visitors, so it makes sense to store form results there because it helps protect the privacy of anyone who fills out the form. Storing it in another publicly accessible folder on your Web can cause privacy problems. Keep the results in _private unless you have a compelling reason to put them elsewhere.

Processing a Form

Once you begin to receive form information from your visitors, you'll probably want to customize the results so that the information comes to you in a clear way. Even if you've already saved the form, identified the form handler, and published the form, you can still customize the form results at any time to make the form useful.

Name and Format the Results File

1 Right-click anywhere in the form, and choose Form Properties from the shortcut menu.

3 From the File Format drop-down list, choose the format in which you'd like to receive the data.

2 Click Options.

4 Check Include Field Names if you want the file to include the names of each field as well as the data.

5 Click OK.

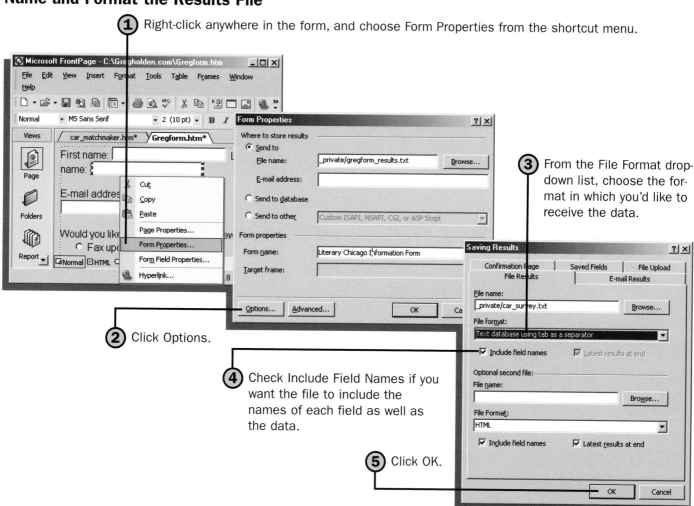

Format E-Mailed Information

1 Right-click the form that has been set up to e-mail results to you, and choose Form Properties from the shortcut menu.

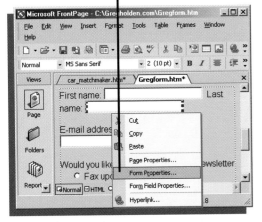

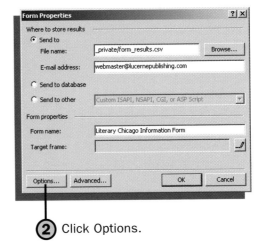

2 Click Options.

3 Click the E-Mail Results tab.

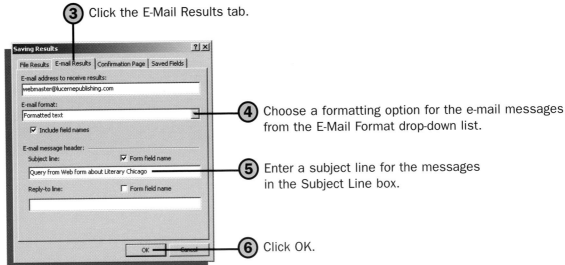

4 Choose a formatting option for the e-mail messages from the E-Mail Format drop-down list.

5 Enter a subject line for the messages in the Subject Line box.

6 Click OK.

Creating a Confirmation Page

After your visitors send you information, you can let them know their submission was successful by using a confirmation form. When the form results arrive at the Web server, the form handler automatically sends this page to the sender, acknowledging the receipt.

Use the Confirmation Page Template

① Open the Web that contains the form you've created.

② Choose Page Or Web from the New submenu of the File menu.

③ Click Page Templates in the Task Pane.

④ Click Confirmation Form, and then click OK.

⑤ Customize the confirmation form by adding your own content.

⑥ Right-click any fields you want to customize, and choose Confirmation Field Properties from the shortcut menu.

⑦ Enter a new name for the field in the Name Of Form Field To Confirm box.

⑧ Click OK.

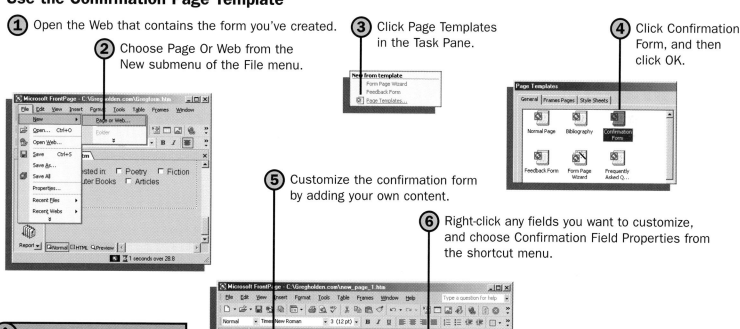

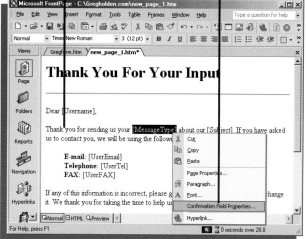

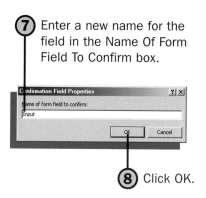

> ⚠ **TIP:** There are two advantages to using the FrontPage Confirmation Page template instead of creating your own page. First, you save yourself some work. Second, FrontPage automatically sets up the confirmation page so that the user input can be displayed. That way the user can make sure the correct information was submitted to you.

Setting Rules for Forms

Simply setting up forms and assigning form handlers to them isn't enough, especially if you're running a business on the Web and it's critical that your customers fill out registration, purchase, and shipping forms accurately. By taking a little extra time to set up rules that users need to follow when they fill out forms (also called forms *validation*), you enable the process of verifying that the forms have been filled out accurately and completely.

Set Rules for Text Boxes

(1) Right-click the text box for which you want to set rules.

(2) Choose Form Field Properties from the shortcut menu.

(3) Click Validate.

(4) Type a name for the field in the Display Name box.

(5) Choose an option from the Data Type drop-down list to constrain the type of content that can be typed in the text box. You can specify text, integer, or number constraints.

!TIP: You can follow the same steps to set up rules for text area boxes as you would for text boxes.

(6) Check Required if you want this to be a required field.

(7) Specify the minimum and maximum number of characters or numbers the text box can contain.

(8) Click OK.

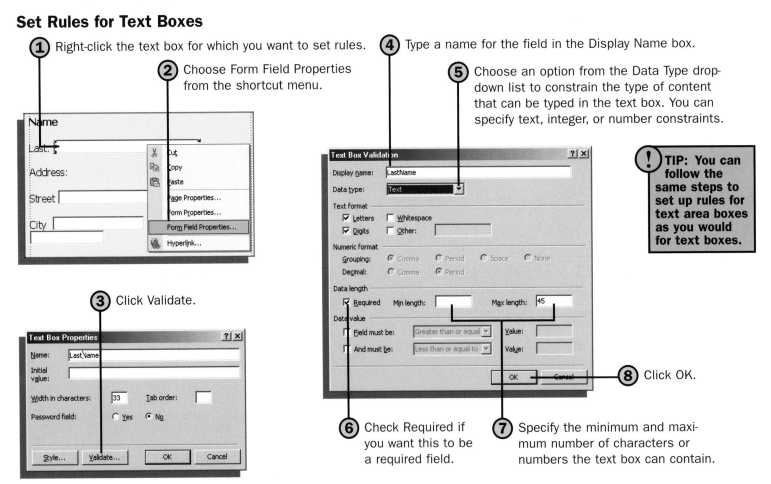

Set Rules for Drop-Down Boxes

(1) Right-click the drop-down menu list that you want to have rules.

(2) Choose Form Field Properties from the shortcut menu.

(3) Click Validate.

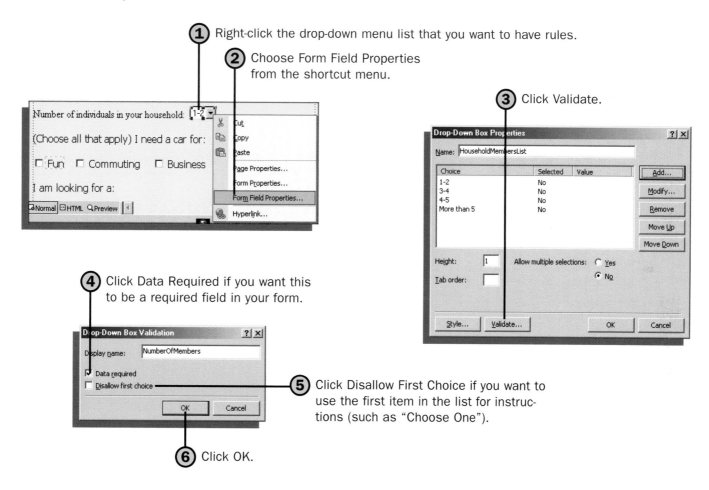

(4) Click Data Required if you want this to be a required field in your form.

(5) Click Disallow First Choice if you want to use the first item in the list for instructions (such as "Choose One").

(6) Click OK.

> **!** **TIP:** You can help ensure that your visitors fill out text boxes or other form fields correctly by suggesting a response in the Initial Value box in the Text Box Properties dialog box.

Administering a Web Site

Many essential administrative tasks take place after you've created and proofread the documents that make up your FrontPage-based Web. This is the stage where you publish your pages on line and make sure your images, links, and forms look and function correctly. The management of a Web site can be a highly technical undertaking—but FrontPage provides the user-friendly tools that make it easy.

Some managerial tasks require you to make changes to individual pages. With FrontPage's help, you can add comments to files and adjust page margins as well as other general properties. Other items in your Webmaster's to-do list occur behind the scenes and are for your benefit rather than for the benefit of your visitors. You can work with a list of tasks you need to complete, you can preview Web pages before they go on line, and you can publish your pages so anyone with a browser can enjoy them. You can also set security parameters for your site, identifying users and groups that are authorized to edit your site and giving visitors the ability to register themselves.

Even after your site goes on line you can use FrontPage to edit pages. In this section, you'll discover how to open a remote Web site and update your pages without ever having to leave FrontPage.

Changing Web and Proxy Settings

If you work in a corporate environment, your company might use a proxy server to provide employees with controlled access to the Internet. If that's the case, you'll need to configure FrontPage to connect to the proxy server so that you can connect to your Web server to publish and edit your pages. You can also set up FrontPage to specify how your FrontPage-based Web should be navigated.

Change Web Settings

① Open the Web that contains the settings you want to change.

② Choose Web Settings from the Tools menu.

③ Enter a new name for your Web in the Web Name box. (This name will be assigned to the folder that holds all the Web's text files, images, and subfolders.)

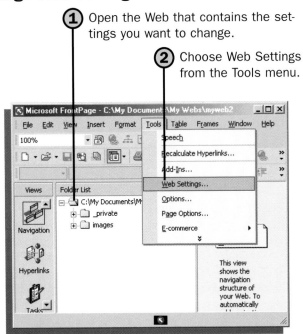

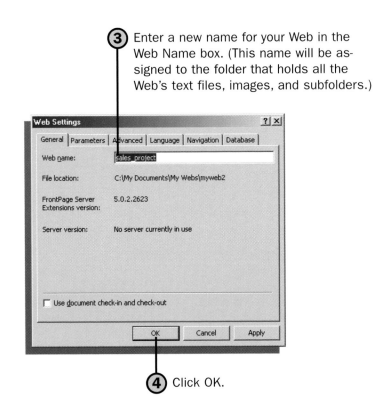

④ Click OK.

Change Navigation Options

(1) Open the Web that contains the settings you want to change.

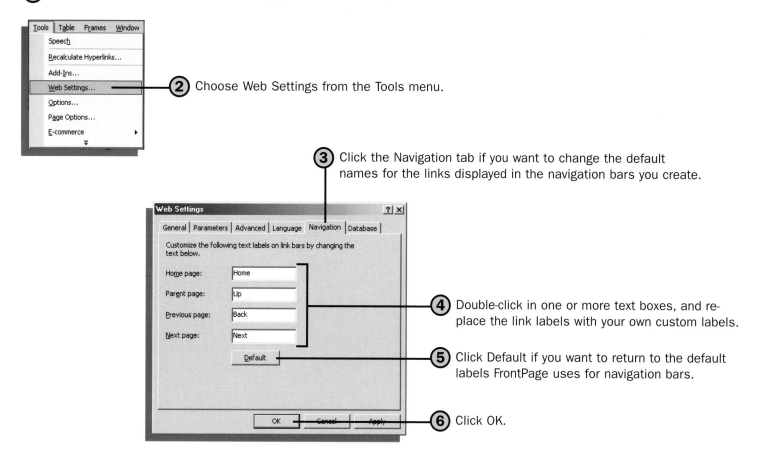

(2) Choose Web Settings from the Tools menu.

(3) Click the Navigation tab if you want to change the default names for the links displayed in the navigation bars you create.

(4) Double-click in one or more text boxes, and re-place the link labels with your own custom labels.

(5) Click Default if you want to return to the default labels FrontPage uses for navigation bars.

(6) Click OK.

TIP: If you want to make a change without closing the Web Settings dialog box, click Apply rather than OK. You can then click another tab and adjust other settings.

CAUTION: When you name a Web page file or folder, keep in mind that the name will be used in a URL on occasion, and URLs cannot contain blank spaces or other special characters. Use the underscore (_) character to indicate a space between words.

Adjust Proxy Settings

① Select Options from the Tools menu.

② Click Proxy Settings.

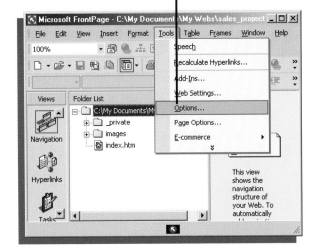

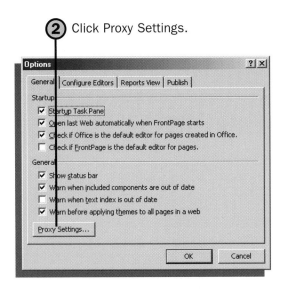

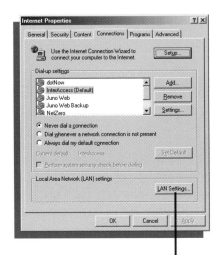

CAUTION: You might think that if you right-click on a Web's name in the Folder List and choose Properties from the shortcut menu, you can open the Web Settings dialog box and change the Web's name. But the Properties dialog box for the Web doesn't let you change the name or other settings. You have to choose Web Settings from the Tools menu to edit the Web's properties.

③ Click LAN Settings to change the settings for your local area network.

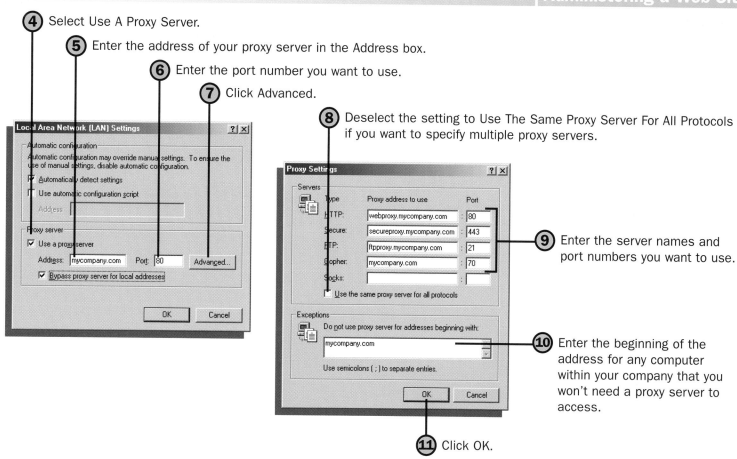

④ Select Use A Proxy Server.

⑤ Enter the address of your proxy server in the Address box.

⑥ Enter the port number you want to use.

⑦ Click Advanced.

⑧ Deselect the setting to Use The Same Proxy Server For All Protocols if you want to specify multiple proxy servers.

⑨ Enter the server names and port numbers you want to use.

⑩ Enter the beginning of the address for any computer within your company that you won't need a proxy server to access.

⑪ Click OK.

TIP: In the Proxy Settings dialog box, the port number you enter depends on the kind of Internet service you want to use. For Hypertext Transfer Protocol communications, you most often would enter port 80. Consult with your network administrator to determine the settings for this and other protocols, such as File Transfer Protocol and Telnet.

CAUTION: Simply configuring FrontPage to connect to your proxy server might not be enough to get you connected to an internal server if you want to publish your FrontPage-based Web there. Some companies also restrict access based on the IP (Internet Protocol) address of the user's computer. Ask your network administrator if your computer needs to be added to the list of approved IP numbers so you can edit and publish pages on your internal Web server.

Annotating a Web Site

Sometimes you need to write notes to yourself or your coworkers about the status of a page you're working on. You can, of course, take a pen and write the message on a sticky note that you attach to your computer screen. But if your colleagues are in another office, it's just as easy to annotate the Web page itself. That way, you can be sure the notes are available when working on your FrontPage-based Web.

Add Comments to a Page

① Position the cursor at the location in the page where you want to add a comment.

② Choose Comment from the Insert menu.

③ Type your comment in the Comment box.

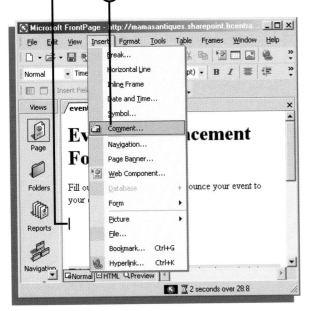

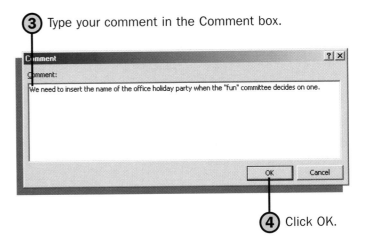

④ Click OK.

! TIP: You can also edit comments by double-clicking them. The Comments dialog box opens immediately, and you don't have to choose Comment Properties from the shortcut menu.

✎ TRY THIS: After you add your comments, click Save and then click Preview. The comments that were visible in Normal view won't be visible. Comments are highlighted in a different color than the visible body text on a Web page. They aren't visible when the page is being viewed by outsiders who access your site with a browser—they are seen only by you and your coworkers when you open the page in FrontPage.

Add Comments About a File

(1) Open the page or Web that contains the file you want to comment on.

(2) Choose Folder List from the View menu if it's not currently displayed.

(4) Click the Summary tab.

(5) Enter your comments in the Comments box.

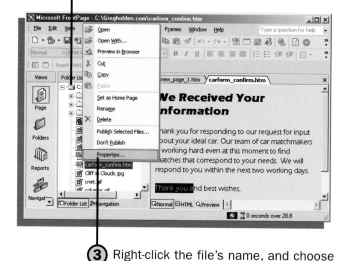

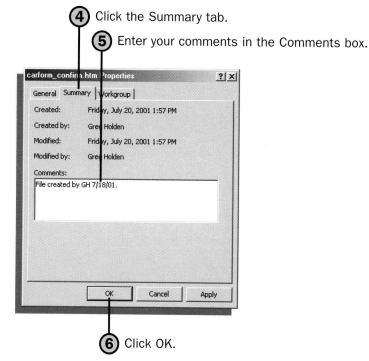

(3) Right-click the file's name, and choose Properties from the shortcut menu.

(6) Click OK.

> **!** **TIP:** You can't add comments in Tasks view. If you need to add comments, you'll need to switch to a different view.

> **!** **TIP:** It's better to use file summary comments when you need to add simple factual information about a file that you or a colleague can view in Reports view. Use comments when you need to make a reminder about a page or a site.

> **SEE ALSO:** File summary comments are only visible in Reports view. You see them when you click Reports in the Views bar. For more information, see "Working with Reports View" on page 209.

Changing Page Settings

You can change a Web page's general properties to make it more readable for your visitors. FrontPage lets you easily make changes that affect a page's overall design as well as content that affects the page as a whole. The Page Properties dialog box contains tools that control a page's title as well as page margins.

Set the General Page Properties

① Right-click the page you want to edit.

② Choose Page Properties from the shortcut menu.

③ Check your title, and enter a new one if you want.

④ Enter a URL to give your visitor's browser the ability to connect to the pages in your Web by using relative URLs. Relative URLs make it easier to update your site if you change servers.

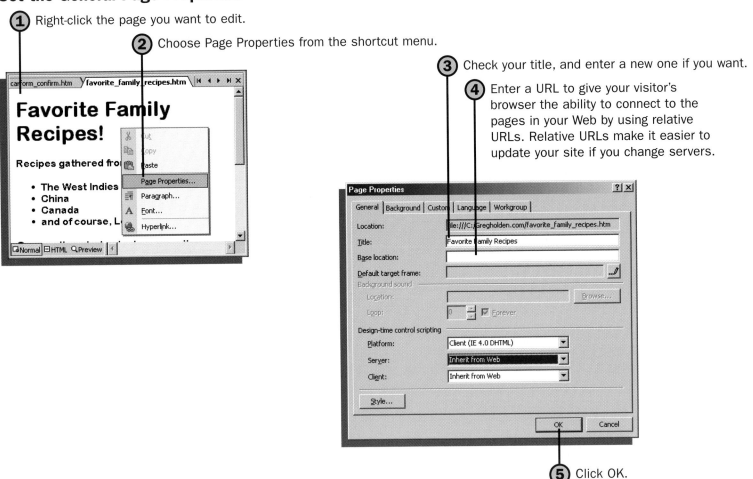

⑤ Click OK.

Set Page Margins

1 Right-click anywhere in the page you want to adjust, and choose Page Properties from the shortcut menu.

2 Click the Margins tab.

3 Select Specify Top Margin to change the page's top margin.

4 Enter a value in pixels.

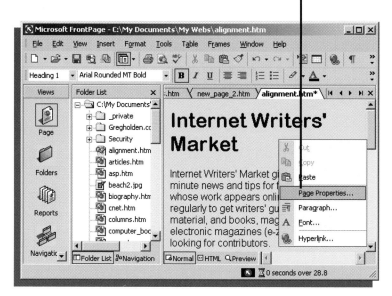

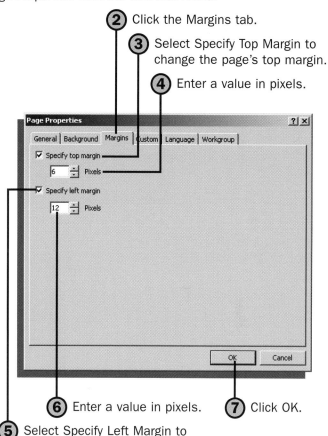

6 Enter a value in pixels.

7 Click OK.

5 Select Specify Left Margin to change the Web page's left margin.

! TIP: You can't change the location or the file name of a page in the General tab of the Page Properties dialog box. You need to choose Save As from the File menu. Then, in the Save As dialog box, you can enter a new file name in the File Name box or choose a new location from the Save In drop-down list.

! TIP: The default top margin is about 21 pixels, and the default left margin is about 12 pixels. If you enter values in the Specify Top Margin or Specify Left Margin box that are less than the default, you'll actually see the page's margins decrease. If you want to increase the margins, enter values that are greater than the default values.

Working with the Task List

Tasks view helps you keep track of the steps involved in completing your FrontPage-based Web. It's useful not only for you, but also for any coworkers or friends who are working on the Web with you. Tasks view doesn't just give you a to-do list of the jobs that remain to be done, however. You can also mark as completed those stages that are finished, so the members of your team can see where you're at and what needs to be addressed next.

Review the Task List

1 Open the Web with the tasks you want to review.

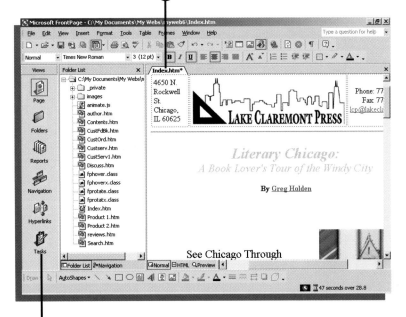

2 Click the Tasks button in the Views bar.

> **TIP:** You can click and drag the dividers between the column headings in the Tasks view (Status, Task, Assigned To, Priority, and so on) to make the columns wider or narrower.

> **CAUTION:** If the task you want to add is associated with the editing of a specific page in your Web, it's better to select that pages's file name in the Folder List and then choose Task from the New submenu of the File menu in order to create a task. Using this technique, the task becomes associated with the file you've selected. You can then start the task by right-clicking its entry in the Tasks view and then selecting Start Task in the shortcut menu. If you right-click the Tasks view area and choose Add Task from the shortcut menu, the task will not be associated with a particular file.

> **TRY THIS:** You can change the order in which tasks are sorted. (By default, FrontPage sorts tasks from highest priority to lowest priority.) To change the sort order, click the Priority heading.

Add a Task

(1) Right-click a blank part of the Tasks view area.

Mark a Task as Complete

(1) Right-click the task.

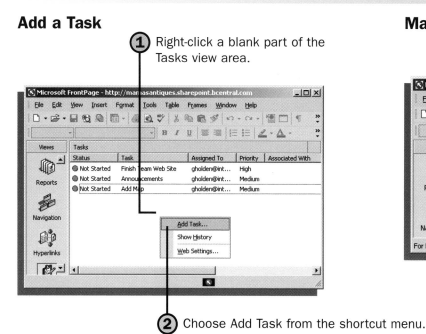

(2) Choose Add Task from the shortcut menu.

(2) Choose Mark Complete from the shortcut menu.

(3) Type a name for the new task in the Task Name box.

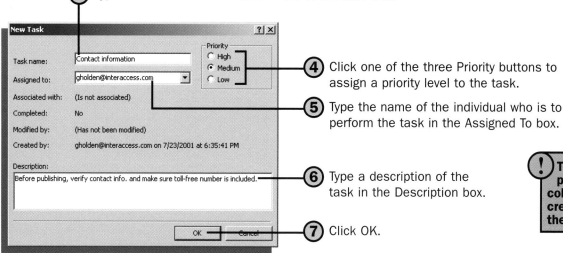

(4) Click one of the three Priority buttons to assign a priority level to the task.

(5) Type the name of the individual who is to perform the task in the Assigned To box.

(6) Type a description of the task in the Description box.

> **TIP:** A page's name only appears in the **Associated With** column in the Tasks view if you create a task after selecting the file name of a page.

(7) Click OK.

Viewing and Editing HTML

FrontPage is flexible enough to enable both novices and experienced programmers to design Web pages the way they want. Beginners can use menus, toolbars, and buttons to weave Web pages. Advanced users can work directly with the source HTML (Hypertext Markup Language) for a Web page.

View HTML Tags

1 Open the page you want to work on.

2 Choose Reveal Tags from the View menu.

3 Pass the mouse pointer over a tag. The entire text of the tag appears as a screen tip.

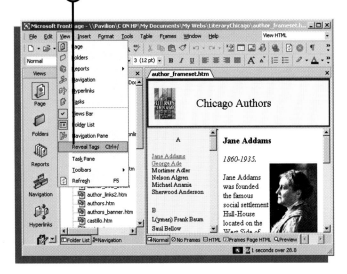

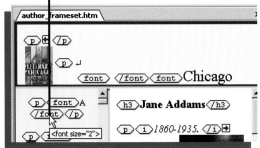

⚠ TIP: You can change the default HTML settings, such as the maximum width of a line of HTML, by choosing Page Options from the Tools menu and then clicking HTML Source. Choose the formatting options you want to change, and then click OK.

⚠ TIP: You can change HTML color coding by choosing Page Options from the Tools menu, clicking the Color Coding tab, and then choosing options from one or more of the drop-down menus to change the color used to highlight a particular type of HTML tag.

Edit HTML

① Click the HTML button to switch to the HTML pane.

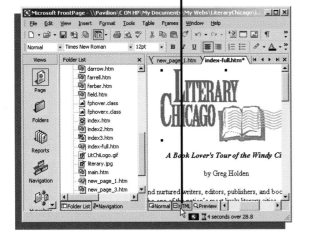

② Position the cursor where you want to modify HTML code.

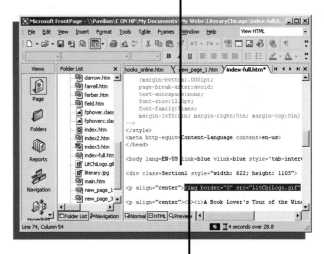

③ Select one or more words, or an entire line of code.

④ Type replacement code, or click Cut, Copy, or Paste to make changes.

TRY THIS: You can add HTML code while working in the Normal pane if you don't want to work in the HTML pane. Position the cursor where you want to insert the code, and then choose Web Component from the Insert menu. Click Advanced Controls in the Component Type list, and then click HTML. Click Finish. In the HTML Markup dialog box, enter the HTML code you want to add, and then click OK.

Verifying Hyperlinks

Broken hyperlinks can quickly undo the experience you've tried so hard to create for visitors to your FrontPage-based Web. Yet links are alarmingly easy to break, especially on complex sites with dozens or even hundreds of pages and an incrementally larger number of links. If you change the location or the name of a file to which other pages are linked, you might need to make the same link change on many pages. FrontPage functions as both a time- and Web-saver by automatically verifying links and recalculating those that need to be replaced.

Verify and Recalculate Hyperlinks

(1) Open the Web site you want to check.

(2) Click Reports on the Views bar.

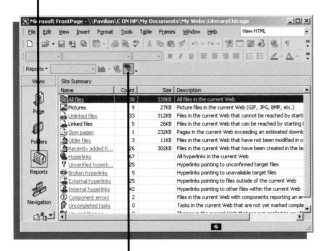

> (!) **TIP:** You don't have to be in Page view to recalculate hyperlinks for your FrontPage-based Web. The Recalculate Hyperlinks command works in all views.

> **TRY THIS:** You can fix a link that is reported to be broken after the verification process. Right-click the hyperlink in Reports view, and then choose Edit Hyperlink from the shortcut menu. You can then enter the correct destination URL for the link in the Replace Hyperlink With box.

(3) In the Reports toolbar, click the Verifies Hyperlinks In The Current Web button.

(4) To correct any broken links, choose Recalculate Hyperlinks from the Tools menu.

Previewing the Web Site

One of the most important aspects of managing a Web site is previewing pages before they go on line and become visible to outsiders. FrontPage gives you two ways to preview pages. You can click the Preview button to preview the page in FrontPage as it would appear in a Web browser, or you can launch your default browser with the current page displayed.

Use the Preview Pane

1 Open the page you want to preview.

2 Click the Preview button.

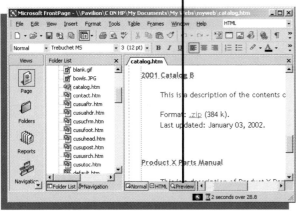

Use a Web Browser

1 Open the page you want to preview, or save changes in any open pages.

2 Click the Preview In Browser button to open the page in your default browser.

CAUTION: Don't use the FrontPage preview function as the last preview for your Web pages. After your pages are published, you need to check them all by opening them in one or more browsers.

TIP: If you haven't saved your page before you click the Preview In Browser button, FrontPage prompts you to do so. You can prevent this prompt from reappearing whenever you want to preview a page by selecting Preview In Browser from the File menu and then selecting Automatically Save Page.

Publishing the Web Site

When you are finished creating content, previewing pages, and verifying hyperlinks, the time comes to move your pages from your own computer to a Web server where they can be accessed by Web surfers. This process is called publishing your Web site. FrontPage makes the publishing process a matter of a few clicks by giving you the Publish Web button right on the toolbar.

Publish a Web to a Server

(1) Open the Web you want to publish.

(2) Click the Publish Web button.

(3) Enter the URL for the Web server where your pages will be stored, or click Browse if you need to locate a server on your local network.

(4) Click OK.

(5) Enter the user name and password you use to access your Web server.

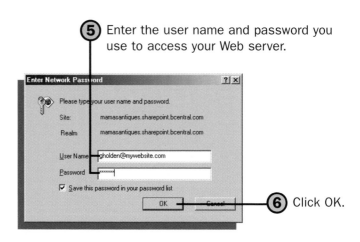

(6) Click OK.

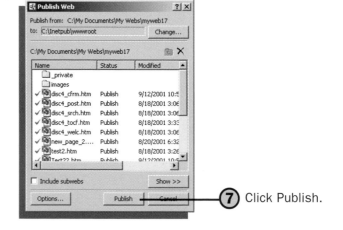

(7) Click Publish.

> ✋ **CAUTION: Make sure there aren't any blank spaces or capital letters in the name of the folder to which you publish your files. Most Web servers run the UNIX operating system, which doesn't work well with blank spaces or capital letters.**

Updating Your Web Site

A FrontPage-based Web is an ongoing project. You need to keep updating and correcting your pages to provide visitors with the most current information available. There's no reason not to update your Web since FrontPage makes updating so easy. You can open a Web site on a remote Web server so that you can make changes as though you're working with files on your own hard disk.

Open a Web to Make Changes

(1) Click the down arrow next to the Open button.

(2) Choose Open Web from the drop-down menu.

(3) Choose one of these options:

- If the Web is on your local computer, locate the Web by clicking the Look In drop-down list.

- If the Web is on another computer, enter its URL in the Web Name box.

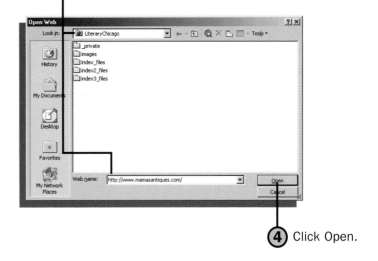

(4) Click Open.

TRY THIS: You can easily mark pages you don't want FrontPage to publish. Right-click the file's name in the Folder List, and then choose Don't Publish from the shortcut menu.

CAUTION: If you are opening a Web that's on a Web server and not on your own computer, FrontPage will prompt you to enter a user name and password so you can access your directory on the server. Have your user name and password ready. You may need to ask your ISP, Web host, or network administrator for instructions on how to obtain a user name and password if you don't have them.

TIP: If you are reopening a Web that you opened recently, choose the Web's name from the Recent Webs submenu of the File menu. FrontPage will connect to the Web automatically without making you locate it in the Open Web dialog box.

Targeting Web Browsers

FrontPage lets you identify which versions of the major browsers you expect your visitors to use and tailors your FrontPage-based Web's contents accordingly. For instance, if you work in a company where only version 3 of Microsoft Internet Explorer is distributed to employees, you can make sure that you don't use advanced content that cannot display correctly in that browser.

Set Browser Compatibility

(1) Open the Web you want to edit.

(2) Choose Page Options from the Tools menu.

(3) Click the Compatibility tab.

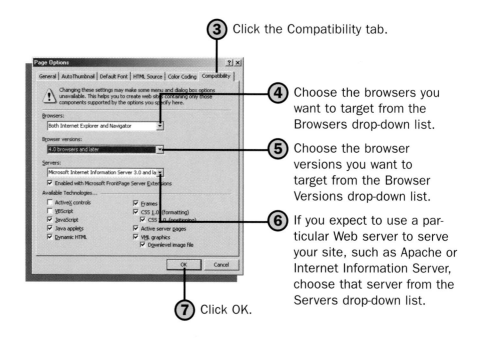

(4) Choose the browsers you want to target from the Browsers drop-down list.

(5) Choose the browser versions you want to target from the Browser Versions drop-down list.

(6) If you expect to use a particular Web server to serve your site, such as Apache or Internet Information Server, choose that server from the Servers drop-down list.

(7) Click OK.

! TIP: If you don't know what server or browser versions will be used to make your pages accessible, you don't need to target them. Just leave the Custom option selected in the Browser Versions drop-down list.

✋ CAUTION: Chances are you'll want to apply your browser compatibility changes to all the pages in your Web. If you select only one page in the Folder List and then select options in the Compatibility tab, the changes will only apply to that one page. To select all the files in a Web, click Folders in the Views bar and then choose Select All from the Edit menu.

Setting User Permissions

Some FrontPage-based Webs aren't intended to be viewed by the public at large, but are restricted to a select group of approved users. In a corporate environment, such Webs can be used for research or other specific projects. To control access to your site, you can create user accounts. These accounts enable specific users or certain computers to connect to your Web.

Connect to Your Permissions Page

① Open the Web you want to restrict.

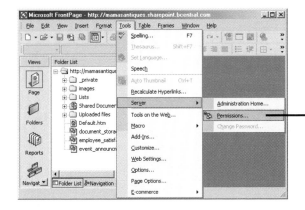

> **⚠ TIP: The instructions shown on these two pages apply to sites that are hosted on a server running Microsoft FrontPage Server Extensions 2002 or SharePoint Team Services. If your server uses Microsoft FrontPage Server Extensions 2000 or earlier, see the FrontPage Help files for instructions.**

② Choose Permissions from the Server submenu of the Tools menu to launch your Web browser, which connects to the Permissions Administration Page for your Web site.

③ Click Manage Users.

④ Click Add A User.

Add a User

1. Type a user name for an individual user to whom you want to grant access.

2. Type a password for the new user.

3. If you want to add an existing user in your workgroup or domain, click Add User Or Group Name.

4. Check one of the boxes in the user role section (Administrator, Advanced Author, Author, Contributor, or Browser) to specify the level of access the new user should have.

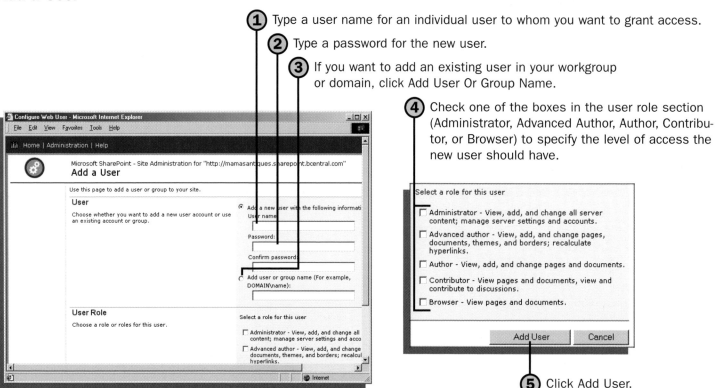

5. Click Add User.

CAUTION: The ability to restrict access to a Web depends on the Web server you are using. Some servers don't let you set up user permissions systems. Check with your network administrator or Web hosting service before you try to restrict access to your site.

Working with Reports View

An important aspect of Web site maintenance is keeping track of your files—who is working with and viewing them, and what problems need to be corrected. With Reports view, you get a detailed set of views of the contents of your FrontPage-based Web. You not only gain the ability to track your site's contents, but you also can connect to a live site on the Internet or an intranet and track its usage.

View the Site Summary

(1) Open the Web whose information you want to view.

(2) Click Reports in the Views bar.

(3) Ensure the Site Summary option is selected in the Reports drop-down menu.

(4) Click on a hyperlinked entry in the Name column to view more specific information about the files mentioned.

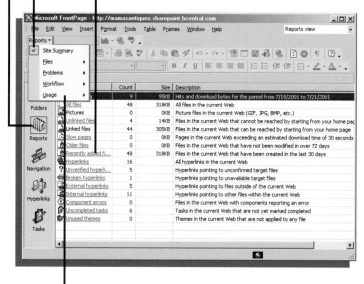

> **! TIP:** Any files you have placed in hidden folders (folders that are preceded by an underscore, such as _private) aren't included in the FrontPage reports, unless you choose Web Settings from the Tools menu, then click the Advanced tab, and then check Show Hidden Files And Folders.

(5) Click the Reports drop-down menu in the Reporting toolbar to switch from one report to another.

> **TRY THIS:** If your Web site reports show more information than you need (or not enough), you can adjust the criteria FrontPage uses to gather the data. Open the Web you want to adjust, and then choose Options from the Tools menu. Click the Reports View tab, and then change the settings as needed.

Check Web Site Usage

(1) Connect to the Web site whose usage you want to check.

(2) Click Reports in the Views bar.

(3) Choose Usage Summary from the Usage submenu of the Reports drop-down list.

(4) Click a hyperlinked item to view more specific information about it.

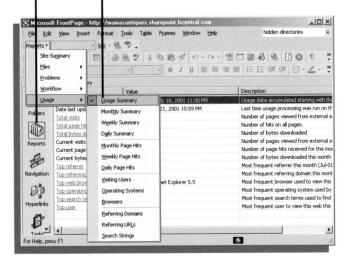

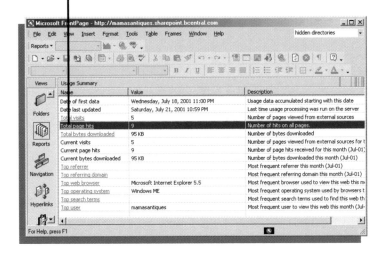

(!) TIP: If you don't see any data in the Usage reports, you may need to activate the usage analysis feature on your server. You need Administrator rights to do this. If you have such rights, select Administration Home from the Server submenu of the Tools menu. Your browser will connect to the Administration home page. Scroll down to the Configure Usage Analysis Settings section, and then click Change Usage Analysis Settings to turn Usage Analysis on.

(!) TIP: In order for FrontPage to provide you with usage statistics, your site needs to be published on a server that supports the Microsoft FrontPage Server Extensions or SharePoint Team Services. You must also have visitors to your site in order to have any statistics to view.

Publicizing Your Web Site to Build Traffic

Part of Web site maintenance is making sure people will come to visit the pages you've worked so hard to create. Few, if any, Web sites generate traffic on their own. Their creators need to reach out and make sure Web surfers are made aware of their site.

bCentral Banner Ad: The bCentral Web components include one feature that can attract visitors. Choose Web Component from the Insert menu and click on bCentral Web Components, and the options shown below appear. By adding this Web component, you join the Banner Ad Network run by Microsoft's Web site hosting service, bCentral. This component enables you to display an ad for a site hosted on bCentral. If you host two ads, you are entitled to have someone else display an ad for your site on theirs.

META tags: You can add special HTML commands (also called *tags*) that increase the chances that your site will show up in response to a search on a search engine. To add such tags to a page, right-click the page and choose Page Properties from the shortcut menu. Click the Custom tag, and then, in the User Variables section, click Add. In the User Meta Variable dialog box, type **Keywords** in the Name box, and then type a series of keywords, each separated by a comma, that describe your site in the Value box, as shown below. Then click OK twice.

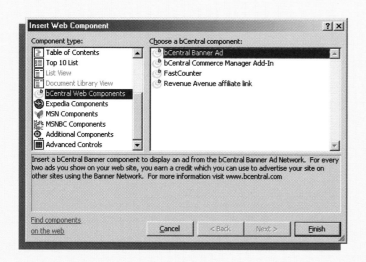

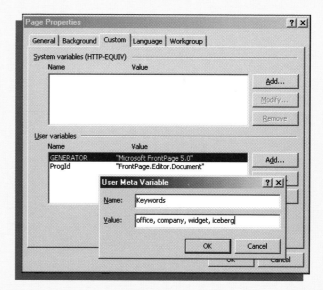

Customizing and Maintaining FrontPage 2002

FrontPage 2002 is all about giving Webmasters like you the tools that match the way you want to work. The Views bar gives you six different ways to view your FrontPage-based Web. The Folder List gives you a hierarchical, Windows Explorer–like guide to your site's contents. If you want a more visual layout, you can switch to the Navigation Pane. You can use the Normal pane if you aren't comfortable with viewing the source HTML for a page. If you like to be in control and understand everything that's going on behind the scenes, on the other hand, you can work in the HTML pane.

But even FrontPage's standard selection of panes, views, toolbars, and menus might not be perfect for your needs. Once you get comfortable with this complex and powerful Web site creation tool, you can assume a higher level of control and customize the program's interface. FrontPage gives users the flexibility to edit and arrange toolbars, menu options, and other parts of its look and feel.

By changing FrontPage's arrangement of tools and options, you can work more quickly and efficiently. You can quickly access those aspects of the program you use most often. In this section, you discover how to customize the FrontPage window, rearrange or even create your own toolbars, add your own images to the FrontPage clip art collections, and alter the colors or other design aspects of themes. Finally you will examine how to repair FrontPage if you encounter problems with the software.

Customizing the FrontPage Program Window

FrontPage gives you a high degree of control over how its main program window looks. You can hide or display the Views bar or change the icons you use to select views. You can also change the appearance and placement of the FrontPage toolbars as well as the status bar, or even add options to a menu bar so you can quickly access the choices you use most often.

Change FrontPage's General Options

(1) Open the Web you want to work on.

(2) Choose Options from the Tools menu.

(3) Select Startup Task Pane if you want the New Document task pane to be displayed automatically when you first start up FrontPage.

(4) Select Open Last Web Automatically When FrontPage Starts if you want FrontPage to open the most recent Web you edited when the program first starts up.

(5) Select Check If FrontPage Is The Default Editor For Pages if you want FrontPage to be your default editor for Web pages.

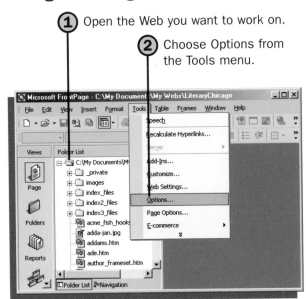

(6) Select Show Status Bar if you want to display the status bar.

(8) Click OK.

(7) Select Warn When Text Index Is Out Of Date if you have created a searchable index for your site that needs to be updated periodically as you create new pages or edit pages.

> **! TIP: Remember that any of the FrontPage toolbars can be detached from the main program window and resized to fit your monitor's display area.**

FrontPage Options You Can Customize

The image below gives you an idea of some of the elements of the FrontPage window you can customize.

Add a new option to any menu.

Tell FrontPage to always display full menus.

Add or remove toolbar buttons.

Use large icons instead of the standard small icons.

Use small icons or hide the Views bar.

Hide or display the status bar.

Add an image to the clip art collection.

Create your own custom toolbar.

Change a theme's colors.

Toggle between the Navigation Pane and the Folder List.

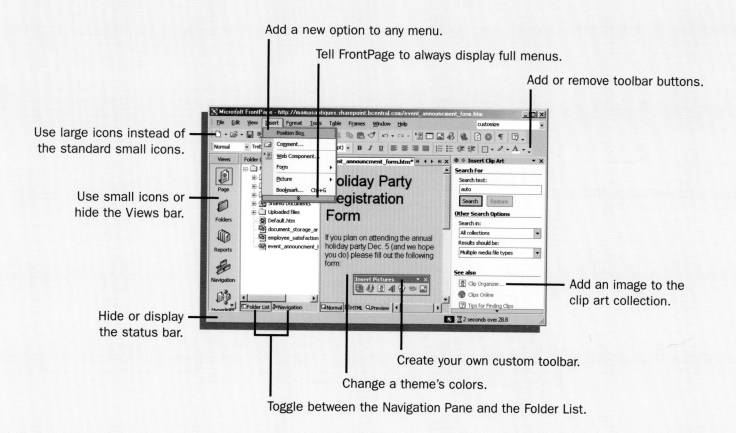

Customizing the FrontPage Toolbars

The Web is all about clicking, whether on buttons or on hyperlinks, and the FrontPage toolbars give you a way to perform many editing functions with individual mouse clicks. Sometimes you need to perform functions that you can access only by using the FrontPage menus. Other times, toolbars will contain more options than you need and take up too much valuable screen space. Adding commands to toolbars and moving or removing buttons can help you work more efficiently.

Add or Remove a Button

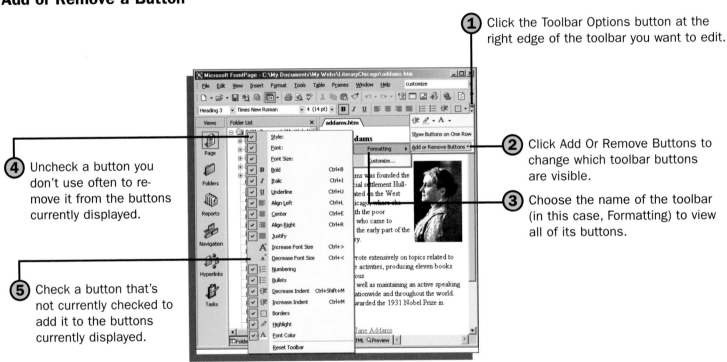

1 Click the Toolbar Options button at the right edge of the toolbar you want to edit.

2 Click Add Or Remove Buttons to change which toolbar buttons are visible.

3 Choose the name of the toolbar (in this case, Formatting) to view all of its buttons.

4 Uncheck a button you don't use often to re-move it from the buttons currently displayed.

5 Check a button that's not currently checked to add it to the buttons currently displayed.

TIP: The Reset Toolbar option that appears at the bottom of the list enables you to reset the toolbar back to its default selection of buttons.

TIP: The Show Buttons On One Row option only appears when you click the Toolbar Options button at the end of the Standard or Formatting toolbar, not other toolbars.

Create Your Own Custom Toolbar

(1) Choose Customize from the Tools menu.

(2) Click New.

(3) Type a name for your new toolbar in the Toolbar Name box.

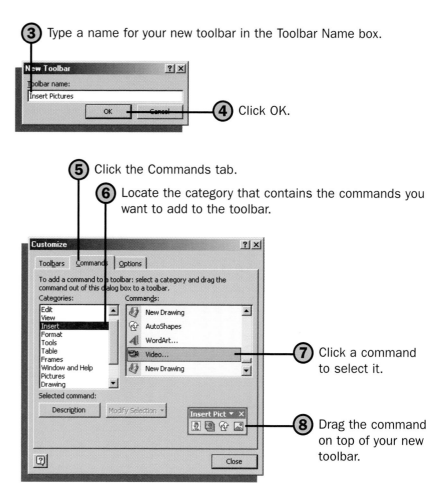

(4) Click OK.

(5) Click the Commands tab.

(6) Locate the category that contains the commands you want to add to the toolbar.

(7) Click a command to select it.

(8) Drag the command on top of your new toolbar.

TRY THIS: You can also drag-and-drop menu commands directly onto a toolbar in the FrontPage window. Open the Customize dialog box and make sure the name of the menu you want to customize is visible in the FrontPage window and not obscured by the dialog box. Select the command on the Commands tab, and then drag it on top of the name of the menu to which you want to add the command.

TRY THIS: The Toolbars tab of the Customize dialog box lists some toolbars in addition to those listed in the Toolbars submenu of the View menu—specifically, 3-D Settings and Shadow Settings. Check these options to view them immediately, and click Close to add them to the Toolbars submenu.

Configuring Editors

You may work with a variety of files on a Web site, including images, spreadsheets, charts, and style sheets. If you need to edit any of these non-Web-page files, you can tell FrontPage which program you want to use as the editor for a particular file type. Then FrontPage will open the file when you want to edit it—for instance, on the General tab of the Picture Properties dialog box, when you click the Edit button, the editor of your choice will automatically launch and open the file.

Specify an Editor

(1) Choose Options from the Tools menu.

(2) Click the Configure Editors tab.

(3) Click Add to add a file type that's not listed in the Type column.

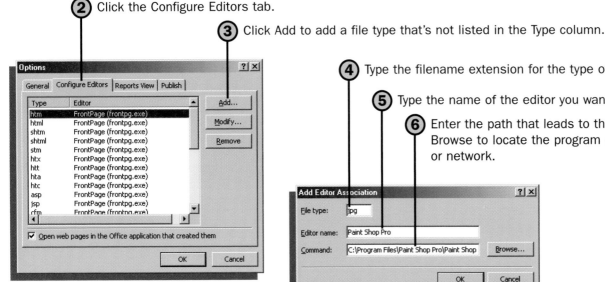

(4) Type the filename extension for the type of file you want to add.

(5) Type the name of the editor you want to use.

(6) Enter the path that leads to the program, or click Browse to locate the program on your computer or network.

(7) Click OK.

> ✋ **CAUTION: You can remove an association between a type of a file and an application by selecting the file type on the Configure Editors tab of the Options dialog box and then clicking Remove. But be careful if you remove an association—FrontPage won't be able to open those files unless you choose another application to open them.**

Modify an Editor

(1) Choose Options from the Tools menu.

(2) Click the Configure Editors tab.

(3) Select the type of file for which you want to define the editor.

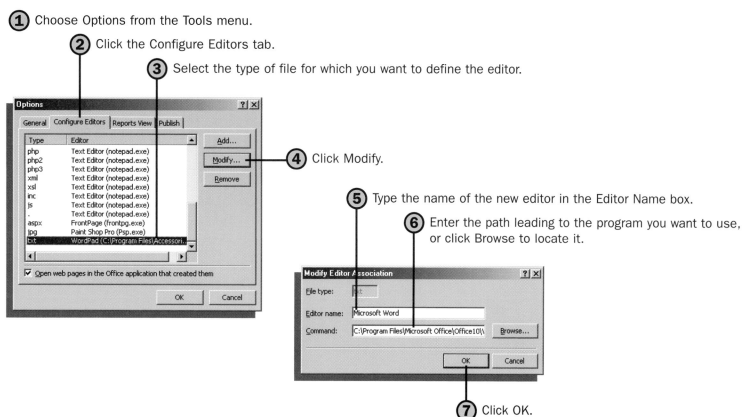

(4) Click Modify.

(5) Type the name of the new editor in the Editor Name box.

(6) Enter the path leading to the program you want to use, or click Browse to locate it.

(7) Click OK.

TRY THIS: Even if you associate a particular type of file with an application, you can still open that file with another application. Right-click the file's name in the Folder List, and then choose Open With from the shortcut menu. Choose the application from the Open With Editor dialog box, which lists all the editors named on the Configure Editors tab of the Options dialog box.

Creating Your Own Clip Art

Although several hundred pieces of clip art are included with FrontPage, you might still want to add your own images to the clip art collections. For instance, you or a coworker might scan your company's logo for use on your Web site. The members of your workgroup can easily access the logo when working on your Web pages if you make it available from the FrontPage Clip Organizer.

Add Your Image

1 Select Clip Art from the Picture submenu of the Insert menu.

2 Click Clip Organizer in the See Also section of the Insert Clip Art task pane.

3 Choose On My Own from the Add Clips To Organizer submenu of the Clip Organizer's File menu.

4 Select one or more files for addition to the Clip Organizer.

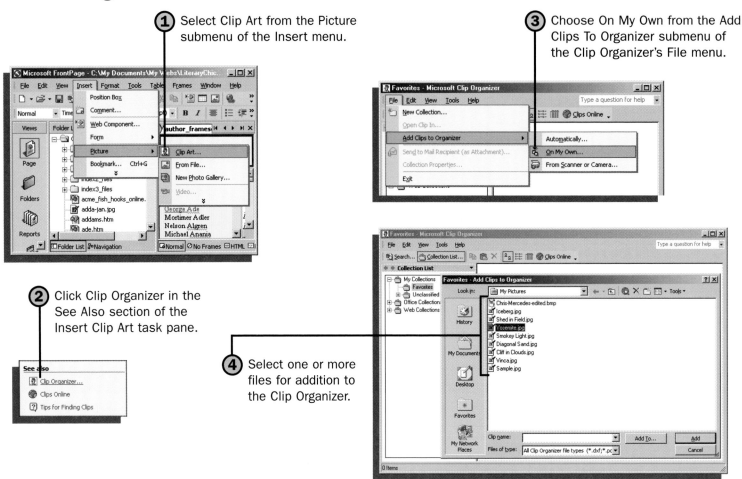

Move an Image to a Clip Art Collection

1 Click the down arrow next to the image as it appears in the right pane of the Clip Organizer, and then choose Move To Collection from the shortcut menu.

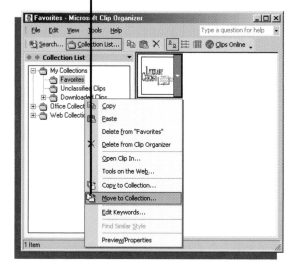

2 Click the name of the collection to which you want to add the image, or click New if you want to create a new collection.

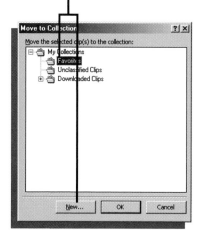

3 If you are creating a new collection, type the name of the new collection in the Name box and then click OK.

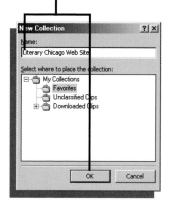

TIP: When you add an image to the clip art collections, the Clip Organizer automatically creates search keywords based on the file's extension and folder name so that you or your coworkers can later find your files easily. By right-clicking on the selected image in the right pane of the Clip Organizer you can select Edit Keywords from the shortcut menu, which then allows you to add new keywords or edit existing keywords.

4 Click OK in the Move To Collection dialog box.

Using Detect and Repair

Occasionally programs such as FrontPage encounter problems that don't result from obvious causes. Some information about the program stored in the Windows Registry might have become corrupted, for instance, or some of the files the software needs to operate might have been accidentally discarded. If you encounter problems running FrontPage, you can use the built-in Detect and Repair application that's common to all Microsoft Office programs.

Fix the FrontPage Program

① Close and save any open files or open Webs.

② Choose Detect And Repair from the Help menu.

③ Leave Restore My Shortcuts While Repairing checked so that you keep a shortcut to FrontPage on the Windows Start menu.

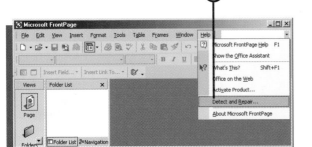

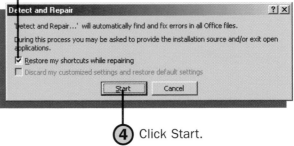

④ Click Start.

✋ CAUTION: If you have customized the FrontPage toolbars, menus, or other aspects of the program, much of your work will be undone when you run Detect and Repair. You'll also need to re-enter your user name and initials when you restart FrontPage after running the repair program.

❗ TIP: Before running Detect and Repair, write down any customization changes you've made to the program so that you can re-create them later on.

Index

Send feedback about this index to *mspindex@microsoft.com*.

_ (underscore), 191, 208
3-D shapes, 217

A

active graphics, 35–37
addresses, Web page and email, 44, 114, 182, 184
administration, 189–211
   annotating Web sites, 194–95
   changing Web and proxy settings, 190–93
   changing Web page settings, 196–97
   previewing Web sites, 203
   publicizing Web sites, 211
   publishing Web sites, 204
   Reports view and, 209–10
   setting user permissions, 207–8
   targeting Web browsers, 206
   Tasks view and, 198–99
   updating Web sites, 205
   verifying hyperlinks, 202
   viewing and editing HTML, 200–201
advanced buttons, 178
alignment. *See also* spacing
   horizontal line, 65
   image, 84–85
   paragraph, 60
Alt+Enter key combination, 87
alternate text, 87, 94
animation, 142, 148
annotating Web sites, 194–95

B

background colors, 89, 134. *See also* colors
background pictures, 35, 36. *See also* images
background sound, 92–93
banner ads, 149, 211
bCentral. *See* Microsoft bCentral
beveling images, 91
blank spaces in names, 204
blank Web pages, 24
BMP (Windows bitmap) format, 72, 79
bold text, 56
bookmarks, 113, 118–19
borders
   cell, 105
   frame, 129, 137
   hyperlink image, 115
   shared, 120–21, 128
   table, 98
   thumbnail, 91
brightness, image, 88, 91
broken links, 202
browsers. *See* Web browsers
bulleted lists, 62
businesses. *See* online businesses

Answer Wizard (column, under B top right)

Answer Wizard, 17, 18, 145
aspect ratios, 83
associations, file, 198, 218, 219
automatic spell-checking, 54
automatic table formatting, 98, 109

buttons
   adding and deleting, 177–79
   creating, from thumbnails, 91
   customizing toolbars and, 216–17
   positioning, 121

C

C++, 171
capital letters, 204
Cascading Style Sheets (CSS), 36
cells
   adding, 100
   adding text and images to, 106
   combining, 105
   deleting, 102
   formatting, 107
   splitting, 104
   tables and, 97 (*see also* tables)
CGI (Common Gateway Interface), 171
characters, case of, 204. *See also* text
charts, 152
check boxes, 179
circular hotspots, 86
clip art. *See also* images
   adding, 73
   customizing, 220–21
   searching for, 73–77
   thumbnail, 90–91
   transparent, 89
Clipboard, 28–29, 50

Windows bitmap (BMP) format, 72, 79
Windows Metafile Format (WMF), 72
Windows Registry, 222
wizards
    Answer, 17, 18, 145
    Create Shortcut, 10
    creating Web sites with, 5, 23, 32–35
    Form Page, 170
    Internet Connection, 14
WMF (Window Metafile Format), 72
workgroups, 163, 174
work-related Web sites, 46
World Wide Web. *See* Web (World Wide Web)
wrapping
    text around images, 85
    word, 44
WWW. *See* Web (World Wide Web)

XML (Extensible Markup Language), 9

zoom options, 125

About the Author

Greg Holden has had Microsoft FrontPage very much on his mind, this book following on the heels of *E-Commerce Essentials with Microsoft FrontPage*, also published by Microsoft Press. Greg cut his computer book-writing teeth in 1995 with *Publishing on the World Wide Web*. Since then he has developed a following with books like *Starting an Online Business for Dummies*. Greg has created online courses on Microsoft Windows 2000 and Microsoft Word 2000, is a regular columnist for CNET, and has written articles for *Forbes, PC World,* and *Computer User.* Outside of the computer world, Greg has published poems, short stories, and, most recently, *Literary Chicago: A Book Lover's Tour of the Windy City,* published by Lake Claremont Press.

When his fingers aren't tapping computer keys or stained with the ink of the antique fountain pens he collects, Greg's hands are busy rehabbing his house on the North Side of Chicago. His greatest joy is not the sound of hammer, saw, or hard disk, but the laughter of his two daughters, Zosia and Lucy.

The manuscript for this book was prepared and submitted to Microsoft Press in electronic form. Text files were prepared using Microsoft Word 2002. Pages were composed by Microsoft Press using Adobe PageMaker 6.52 for Windows, with text set in Times and display type in ITC Franklin Gothic. Composed pages were delivered to the printer as electronic prepress files.

Cover Graphic Designer

Tim Girvin Design

Interior Graphic Designers

Joel Panchot, James D. Kramer

Interior Graphic Artist

Michael Kloepfer

Principal Compositor

Kerri DeVault

Principal Proofreader/Copy Editor

Holly M. Viola

Indexer

Shane-Armstrong Information Systems

Your *fast-answers, no jargon* guides to Windows XP and Office XP

Get the fast facts that make learning the Microsoft® Windows® XP operating system and Microsoft Office XP applications plain and simple! Numbered steps show exactly what to do, and color screen shots keep you on track. *Handy Tips* teach easy techniques and shortcuts, while quick *Try This!* exercises put your learning to work. And *Caution* notes help keep you out of trouble, so you won't get bogged down. No matter what you need to do, you'll find the simplest ways to get it done with PLAIN & SIMPLE!

Microsoft Windows® XP Plain & Simple
ISBN 0-7356-1525-X

Microsoft Office XP Plain & Simple
ISBN 0-7356-1449-0

Microsoft Word Version 2002 Plain & Simple
ISBN 0-7356-1450-4

Microsoft Excel Version 2002 Plain & Simple
ISBN 0-7356-1451-2

Microsoft Outlook® Version 2002 Plain & Simple
ISBN 0-7356-1452-0

Microsoft FrontPage® Version 2002 Plain & Simple
ISBN 0-7356-1453-9

Microsoft Access Version 2002 Plain & Simple
ISBN 0-7356-1454-7

U.S.A.	**$19.99**
Canada	**$28.99**

Microsoft
microsoft.com/mspress

Target your problem and
fix it yourself—
fast!

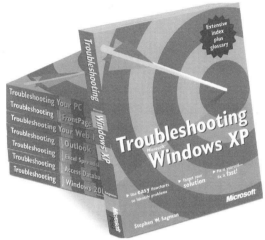

When you're stuck with a computer problem, you need answers right now. *Troubleshooting* books can help. They'll guide you to the source of the problem and show you how to solve it right away. Get ready solutions with clear, step-by-step instructions. Go to quick-access charts with *Top 20 Problems* and *Preventive Medicine*. Find even more solutions with handy *Tips* and *Quick Fixes*. Walk through the remedy with plenty of screen shots. Find what you need with the extensive, easy-reference index. Get the answers you need to get back to business fast with *Troubleshooting* books.

Troubleshooting Microsoft® Office XP
ISBN 0-7356-1491-1

Troubleshooting Microsoft® Access Databases
(Covers Access 97 and Access 2000)
ISBN 0-7356-1160-2

Troubleshooting Microsoft® Access Version 2002
ISBN 0-7356-1488-1

Troubleshooting Microsoft Excel Spreadsheets
(Covers Excel 97 and Excel 2000)
ISBN 0-7356-1161-0

Troubleshooting Microsoft Excel Version 2002
ISBN 0-7356-1493-8

Troubleshooting Microsoft® Outlook®
(Covers Microsoft Outlook 2000 and Outlook Express)
ISBN 0-7356-1162-9

Troubleshooting Microsoft Outlook Version 2002
(Covers Microsoft Outlook 2002 and Outlook Express)
ISBN 0-7356-1487-3

Troubleshooting Your Web Page
(Covers Microsoft FrontPage® 2000)
ISBN 0-7356-1164-5

Troubleshooting Microsoft FrontPage Version 2002
ISBN 0-7356-1489-X

Troubleshooting Microsoft Windows®
(Covers Windows Me, Windows 98, and Windows 95)
ISBN 0-7356-1166-1

Troubleshooting Microsoft Windows 2000 Professional
ISBN 0-7356-1165-3

Troubleshooting Microsoft Windows XP
ISBN 0-7356-1492-X

Troubleshooting Your PC
ISBN 0-7356-1163-7

microsoft.com/mspress

Tune in and turn on to the *ultimate*

digital media

experience!

U.S.A. **$29.99**
Canada $43.99
ISBN: 0-7356-1455-5

Listen to Internet radio. Watch breaking news over broadband. Build your own music and video playlists. With the MICROSOFT® WINDOWS MEDIA® PLAYER FOR WINDOWS® XP HANDBOOK, you control the airwaves! Personalize the way you see, hear, and experience digital media with this all-in-one kit of tools and how-tos from the Microsoft Windows Media team. You get everything you need to bring cutting-edge music and video everywhere your PC, laptop, or portable device goes!

microsoft.com/mspress

Self-paced

training that works as hard as you do!

Information-packed STEP BY STEP courses are the most effective way to teach yourself how to complete tasks with the Microsoft® Windows® XP operating system and Microsoft® Office XP applications. Numbered steps and scenario-based lessons with practice files on CD-ROM make it easy to find your way while learning tasks and procedures. Work through every lesson or choose your own starting point—with STEP BY STEP'S modular design and straightforward writing style, *you* drive the instruction. And the books are constructed with lay-flat binding so you can follow the text with both hands at the keyboard. Select STEP BY STEP titles also provide complete, cost-effective preparation for the Microsoft Office User Specialist (MOUS) credential. It's an excellent way for you or your organization to take a giant step toward workplace productivity.

- **Microsoft Windows XP Step by Step**
  ISBN 0-7356-1383-4

- **Microsoft Office XP Step by Step**
  ISBN 0-7356-1294-3

- **Microsoft Word Version 2002 Step by Step**
  ISBN 0-7356-1295-1

- **Microsoft Excel Version 2002 Step by Step**
  ISBN 0-7356-1296-X

- **Microsoft PowerPoint® Version 2002 Step by Step**
  ISBN 0-7356-1297-8

- **Microsoft Outlook® Version 2002 Step by Step**
  ISBN 0-7356-1298-6

- **Microsoft FrontPage® Version 2002 Step by Step**
  ISBN 0-7356-1300-1

- **Microsoft Access Version 2002 Step by Step**
  ISBN 0-7356-1299-4

- **Microsoft Visio® Version 2002 Step by Step**
  ISBN 0-7356-1302-8

Microsoft Press® products are available worldwide wherever quality computer books are sold. For more information, contact your book or computer retailer, software reseller, or local Microsoft Sales Office, or visit our Web site at microsoft.com/mspress. To locate your nearest source for Microsoft Press products, or to order directly, call 1-800-MSPRESS in the United States. (in Canada, call 1-800-268-2222).

Prices and availability dates are subject to change.

Microsoft

microsoft.com/mspress